I0080173

Stupid Brain

The Life of a Minor Attracted Person

by James Peak

Editors: Russell Rowland, Maxwell P. Sinsheimer

Stupid Brain
The Life of a Minor Attracted Person

Library of Congress Control Number: 2022921534
ISBN: 979-8-9873273-0-2 (print)
 979-8-9873273-1-9 (e-book)

Copyright 2022 James H. Peak
P.O. Box 21137
Billings, MT 59104

www.stupidbrain.com

All Rights Reserved. No part of this publication may be reproduced, scanned, uploaded, stored in a retrieval system, or transmitted, in any form or by any means, electronic, mechanical, photocopying, recording, or otherwise, without the written permission of the author.

Contents

To my beloved Frannie

Disclaimer

I have tried very hard to make this book honest.

That does not mean it is completely true.

This is the story as I remember it, knowing that memory is not nearly as accurate as it thinks. All of us tell ourselves a story about our life. We think we encode our memories in photographic detail without error or inconsistency, but studies on "eyewitness" accounts suggests that our memory is more suspect than we wish to believe.

This work attempts honesty regarding my lived experience, but I do not vouch for perfect historical accuracy, and I know the passage of time and emotions color and distort how we perceive our reality.

I apologize in advance to family members, friends, and fellow spiritual travelers who share these biographical events but may perceive them very differently.

One does not become enlightened by imagining figures of light, but by making the darkness conscious. The latter procedure, however, is disagreeable and therefore not popular.

   —CG Jung

Little baby

I am a poor boy too

I have no gift to bring

That's fit to give our King.

Shall I play for you?

   —**The Little Drummer Boy**

At the Last Assizes it will acquit.

   —**Herman Melville,** *Billy Budd*

Mortality is the clearest evidence for a benevolent Providence.

   —JP

Chapter 1

Cleveland

The only clear consequence of spending my preschool years in suburban Cleveland was to develop a life-long affection for its cursed sports teams.

I am named after my father, who was in turn named after his. Our shared middle name is Hamilton, after the doctor that delivered my grandfather. My dad kept it for me because it sounded regal, although it did not change the fact that our origins spring from Appalachia. In its post-war glory days, the city's nickname was "Best Location in the Nation." But for my father it was the "Mistake by the Lake." He was so glad to leave Cleveland in the late 1960s. By then, the whole area was simmering with racial animosity and urban decay, but I think it had lost its allure for my father long before the Hough and then the Cuyahoga burned.

James Hamilton Peak Sr.'s family were of Scotch-Irish stock. The grandfather I never met was described as a thin, even scrawny man, but his dashing suits and innate charm betrayed his true nature as a dandy and a ladies' man. Back in Kentucky, the family's business was construction. The Peaks helped level and pave the country back roads that would ultimately service Fort Knox. Coincidentally, my father would be stationed there on the day I was born, February 22, 1962. Construction work was hard and jobs scarce, and in the early 1930s my grandfather Peak happily made the migration north from rural Elizabethtown ("E-Town") to the bright industrial lights of thriving metropolitan Cleveland. Accompanying him was my grandmother Donna Mae Peak, or as I always referred to her, "Nana." Legend had it that back in E-Town her family ran a saloon with bare dirt floors. Men were purported to have died in that saloon.

My Aunt Clara was born in 1924. I imagine Dad appeared as something of a surprise in 1937. My father passed away while I was in prison. I had finally made it to treatment just prior to my sentencing, and as I tried to trace the catastrophe that my life had become, I was eager for what crumbs of family history my father could recall, as he rarely mentioned it on his own. His memory was of a sometimes loving, sometimes tempestuous relationship between his parents. His father loved to dress up and hit the town. At times James Sr. would come home late, his evening whereabouts uncertain. Fights ensued, and Dad remembers Nana flinging a skillet of hot grease in his father's general direction. There were precious few shared interactions between father and son, and I think that void reverberated in my family for several generations. Dad does remember the two of them sharing a mock air battle between the "Yanks" and the "Japs" soon after Pearl Harbor, but I think my missing grandfather was a ghostly presence even when alive.

Due to a mild physical disability, James Sr. did not join the Armed Forces during World War II. He worked himself up to chief cashier for Cleveland Metropolitan Transport. His final task one afternoon in 1943 was to collect that day's fares and deposit them in the bank. On the way he was accosted by three men, one Italian, one Pole, and one Negro. This is how my father remembers it, like a bad ethnic joke. They shot my grandfather for the collected fares. He died two days later. All three murderers went to the chair.

My father never forgot the funeral at Fairlawn Cemetery; the long, long rows of limousines, crowds of somber men in hats and suits. He acutely recalled "colored" railroad porters appearing in force to offer condolences for a man they respected, a rare crossing of the color barrier at that time. The last thing he remembers is a picture of his seven-year-old self on the front page of the *Cleveland Plain Dealer* with the caption "Left Behind." My father hated how the paper traded on his personal sorrow. He refused to read it as an adult.

Of course, lots of kids became fatherless, or motherless, or both in those days. But my Nana, Donna Mae Peak, was not the typical post-war single mother. Donna loved to dress in pink to reassure others of her femininity. But years before her husband's death she had started selling real estate on her own, outearning her spouse, a secret she was careful *not* to keep. She was the dominant force in their marriage and became the first female president of the Cleveland Board of Realtors, a remarkable achievement for the time, and a testament to her drive and ambition.

Donna Mae was a loving but imperious and demanding woman who brooked little opposition from her husband or his surviving son. Nana did not think much of my dad's innate ability and suggested a safe, secure career as a mortician. Although he was told by his principal at Shaw High School that he was not college material, Dad nonetheless managed to escape the powerful gravitational pull of my grandmother and left Cleveland in the middle of the academic year to attend college downstate at Ohio Wesleyan; anything to get the hell out and be on his own.

There he met my mother Janith Elaine Root of Erie, Pennsylvania. Her parents were Kenneth and Anne. I remember my grandfather as a dignified man, proud of his genealogy which he claimed, if it did not go back to the *Mayflower*, came within shooting distance. It was only many years later that I learned Grandfather's patrician roots sprang more from the furniture manufacturing mill town of Cory, Pennsylvania than from Plymouth Rock. As the oldest son, it would be his responsibility to retrieve his father's body from whatever ditch it had fallen into after the evening's festivities. Sometime during the early years of the Depression, he met Anne Smith, whose family had escaped from the Oklahoma Dust Bowl. Scandalously they eloped. I tried to ask about it once and was rewarded with deafening silence and my grandfather's gorgon stare. Grandpa Root worked as a janitor to pay his way through Ohio State, eventually earning an accounting degree. He became a thoroughly respectable man in a thoroughly respectable profession, a Shriner, and a pious Methodist.

All I remember is that he was the dullest, most sober man to ever live. Joy was sucked out of the room like a vacuum whenever he entered. He possessed the mental flexibility of a horizontal line. As a ten-year-old, I remember stumbling upon reams of paper from the 1950s, wrapped and stacked as carefully as $100 bills, stored incomprehensibly in one of several basement freezers. I later learned that it was a copy of every check the man had ever written. I believe the chilly air was meant to ward off time's decay.

Later, when I was in medical school, we spent an indelible afternoon reviewing the archives of the many comprehensive gastrointestinal consultations he had obtained from every chairman of internal medicine for a thousand miles. As best as I could determine, the cause for his sputtering, temperamental intestines had baffled the best medical minds of his generation. He hoped that later I might be tempted into an inquiry of my own.

How my grandmother Anne got stuck with Kenneth was beyond me. She was sharp, funny, and independent. They quarreled constantly and slept not just in separate bedrooms, but on separate floors. As experienced combatants, my grandparents developed wounding verbal skills of thrust and parry that always left a mark but never succeeded in ending the life-long conflict. My mother developed a wonderful strategy to deal with never-ending marital conflict; she pretended it was not there. By second grade, she had learned how to maneuver the Erie City bus system and spent every spare minute after class playing at the Downtown YMCA. In the 1940s and 50s it was not considered child neglect for an elementary school kid to take off after school and play in the fields, swim at Presque Isle, or travel into town without constant adult supervision. Progress has since intervened, and no doubt Child Protective Services would be called if a seven-year-old child were unaccompanied on a city bus.

Mom's younger sister Carol was a much more sensitive child less inclined towards independence than Jan, and as a result was traumatized by the constant carping and infighting between my grandparents. Even after fifty years it is a subject my aunt cannot bring up without tears. In any case, Mom grew up seemingly content and unperturbed by the marital unhappiness around her, but she was determined to avoid such a fate happening to her when she became a bride.

My parents found each other at Ohio Wesleyan University, and soon after they married, fate and Khrushchev intervened in the form of the Berlin Crisis, which resulted in my father being drafted. He and his young bride were stationed at Fort Knox, less than twenty miles from where he grew up. I was born at the Ireland Army Hospital there on Feb. 22, 1962. Fortunately, the Crisis was short-lived, and we soon moved back to the Cleveland area.

I have one singular memory of my pre-school years in Elyria. I was four, in bed, trying to rock myself to sleep. But before I finally collapsed, I would amuse myself by closing my eyes so tightly so I could see bursts of bright light reflected against my closed eyelids. By my toddler logic, it mimicked the stars in heaven. This night, in a dream, I saw just one incandescently bright light that I instinctively knew was celestial: God beckoning me in a kind and loving way. How a four-year-old would know such things is a mystery. I just knew. I also understood as loving as the light was, that once I joined it, I would be called from this world, and would have to leave my Mommy. I fought the light; Mommy was more important to me than God. I awoke, escaping the light, but with my eyes wide open I wondered if I had denied God and made a horrible mistake. It would be 45 years before I had any other spiritual experience like that.

My father worked in middle management for an auto parts manufacturer. He was restless for a better future, and the late sixties was the era of the company man and promotions. Mayflower moving vans were a common sight in our neighborhood. Everyone was chasing the suburban dream. Dad was also eager to leave the integrating, and therefore combustible city of Cleveland. Just before I started first grade my family, now including my two younger brothers David and John, left Ohio for the bucolic, rural town of Simsbury, Connecticut.

A part of my heart will always be at 19 Chestnut Hill Road, for I had many happy times there. We moved into a brand-new subdivision where an old apple orchard had been. The streets were wide and uncrowded, curving through the rolling landscape below West

Mountain. There were wonderful bike paths weaving in and out of the trees behind the rows of faux colonials. Our backyard was over an acre, practically a continent to a six-year-old, and I knew every inch.

Memory is a curious thing. There are whole swaths of my thirties and forties that feel like a grey blob of undifferentiated recollections, but first grade through early adulthood is etched in crystal, for good and bad. On my deathbed, I doubt I will know where I am, but I will be able to draw a fully accurate map of Simsbury circa 1972, the town's tricentennial. In my mind's eye I see riotously colored fall leaves and hear the crackling they make when I jump into a pile. I visualize Sugar Loaf Mountain where we always bought our Christmas trees, covered with fresh snow and warranting its namesake. My brothers and I swam in Town Pond, squishing gelatinous algae under our toes, played Army and kickball in the spacious backyards, and spent a week every summer renting a cottage on a nearby lake. It was as idyllic as it sounds.

I attended Tootin' Hills Elementary, so named because it was located adjacent to an abandoned railroad bed. I could read before kindergarten and loved math and history. Anything requiring manual dexterity, on the other hand, was infinitely more challenging. We all daubed finger paintings the first day of kindergarten. When the mothers came to pick their kids up my teacher Mrs. Schauff showed all the parents our creations, noting "Jenny painted her family, Joey made a rainbow, and Jimmy, well Jimmy is still experimenting with color."

I loved first grade. I got to read and play. Everyone got along, no one was mean. There were three recesses where you could do or play anything you wanted, like tag or house. Afterward I would explore the woods and look for polliwogs and minnows in the ponds. My love for the gentle New England landscape with its brooks and streams and hills bordered on the ecstatic. As a topography, it always seems like home, no matter how long I have strayed from its borders. My adopted state is glorious Montana, and I yield to no one regarding it being the most spectacular place of all. But sometimes Montana feels almost too savage and wild for comfortable human habitation, dry coulees and buttes in the east, the forbidding Rockies in the west. By contrast, Connecticut always had the right size and scale for me, big enough to explore, but never too big to get lost in or intimidated.

It was an Ozzie and Harriett Norman Rockwell early childhood, and I am so grateful for it. In a second, I am mentally transported back to Stratton Brook or Talcott Mountain. There I am lying in the grass, making a fort, listening to the birds, and touching the sticky sap of the big old white pines that surround our house.

At the time, Mom was perfect, loving, and warm. My father came from a much more emotionally distant place. He had grown up without a father in a home dominated by women. He adored my mother, but she was the only person he ever trusted, and she was just about the only person he ever wanted to be around. His job was to work hard to support the family and provide his boys with a positive male role model. This was more than he ever got, and it was all society expected of him. I am not sure he really liked kids; I am not sure he really liked me, which was heartbreaking because I needed him so much.

I so wanted to make him proud. When in a good mood, he was funny, generous, and strong. After I had put on my pajamas the last thing he would do before my bedtime was to give me a kiss and let me rub his scratchy cheek on my smooth one. It was the highlight of my evening.

Every day he worked hard for lesser men who were his superior due to family and political connections. For years, after a full day in the office, he would drive to Hartford to attend night classes at UConn Law, and he spent many weekend hours studying for the bar. But once home, he mostly wanted to be left alone.

We had a few shared rituals like watching roller derby on Saturday morning (Charlie O'Connell and the Bay City Bombers) or washing his beloved dark brown Lincoln Continental (mom called it the "Turdmobile"). But we never played catch, never went camping or fishing, never really did anything together. I do not know that it bothered me that much at the time, again the deal was Dad earns the living, Mom does everything else. The problem was that this whole guy thing was really a mystery to me, and his emotional absence made it harder.

In first grade, my teachers told me I could no longer play "house" with the girls and needed to start hanging out with the boys. But I did not like the boys as much; they were rough and mean. I just played by myself on the swings and daydreamed. If there was a book on how to be a boy, I would have devoured it instantly, but no such luck. Everything bewildered me. For example, I did not understand how to use a public urinal, and on the first day of school just dropped trousers to the epic delight of my compatriots.

Mom was my world, and I adored her. She was kind, practical and patient, made ginger cookies, ferried the kids to the swimming hole, and smoothed over conflict. If I ever did accomplish anything positive in life it is because of her love.

By first grade I had two younger brothers—David was four and John was a toddler. At dinnertime we all gathered to share the adventures of our day. On schooldays, I worked the room like a press secretary, highlighting my obedience while tattling on the misbehavior of the bad boys. Being "good" was important to me, and I was obedient to obsequiousness. Sometimes the big kids would roughhouse on the bus, inciting the driver to pull over and tell the hooligans she would not move one inch until they quieted. This made me frantic. What if they never shut up? What if I had to stay on the school bus forever? I arrived home distraught, and Mom called the school to make sure it did not happen again.

Rules were not just rules; they were laws, basically commandments, and to disobey felt like madness. I had a strange need to avoid conflict or "being caught" at all costs. Any misbehavior in Mrs. Barkus's third-grade classroom was punished by an ear pull and after school detention. To not be allowed to go home after class was conceptually terrifying. I tolerated physical pain fine and remember cutting my big toe on a piece of glass in a lake, bleeding everywhere and enduring stitches without much fuss, but I was unnaturally terrified of bullies, giving them a power and influence they neither had nor deserved. My father correctly perceived this avoidance as physical cowardice, unmanly and soft. It was my first inkling of what he despised in me.

Physical therapy and occupational therapy would have helped, but nobody knew what those were at the time. All I knew was that my lack of coordination was appalling and embarrassing. I seemed incapable of catching balls, a critical social skill for boys in those days, although I was able to arrest their forward momentum with my face. I was about seven when I learned how to tie my shoelaces, and the only criticism on my report card was to note that my handwriting was generally indecipherable.

Hours were spent in fantasy while gazing at maps and pouring through encyclopedias. I read everything and would stay up past my bedtime reading with just my nightlight. I bought Audubon identification guides for trees and flowers and categorized all the species in our neighborhood. At seven I was dangerous at Jeopardy! (The answer is: It is the second largest city in Japan. What is "Yokohama?" Mais oui). My teacher called me "the Little Professor," and I am not sure it was a compliment. I wished I had more all-around boy skills, but I just had hopeless and vaguely effeminate nerd skills. It might have been cute in *Young Sheldon*, but it was not so endearing in Nixon-era Simsbury.

And I had a weird, secret side I knew even as a second grader was atypical. Lois Lenski wrote a book called *Indian Captive*, about a white girl being kidnapped from her family by Seneca Indians, and I was obsessed with this book. Initially terrified, she comes to see them as her real family. I often imagined myself kidnapped by Indians and tied up (why was tying up part of it?). I loved my family but sensed that I did not belong. This was not my real tribe. I was born into the wrong one.

The serious nature of my confusion was clarified one Saturday morning. I might have been six, my little brother David would have been four.

I remember the setting so well. I was sitting cross-legged (what we called "Indian style" in those less sensitive times) on the brown shag carpet in the room David and I shared. Our record player was on the right side of the room. The window facing Watch Hill Road and West Mountain was on the left, with our twin beds directly in front of us. Various Lincoln Logs and Tonka Trucks were scattered on the floor. What we were doing is less clear to me. We were naked. We were laughing. I believe I was looking at his penis and he was looking at mine. Was I touching his penis? I do not think so, but I am not sure, although whatever I was or was not doing was innocent. What I do know is that my father appeared in our doorway, took one look at us, face instantaneously flushed, clearly furious (at me? us?). He thundered exactly one phrase: "Don't *ever* let me catch you doing that again," then slammed the door shut and fled.

I had never known him to be so angry with me. I was startled, aghast, confused, but mostly ashamed. Dad was a distant but benign planet in our household universe, with limited interest in any of our activities. David once made him so angry he tore about the house to catch and spank him, which was terrifying, but I had no previous memory of him raising his voice to me. We had done something very wrong— the most wrong thing I had ever done in my short life. I never realized I could make my father so angry, and so disappointed. It seemed to have something to do with nudity and my brother. Was it looking, touching, or just being naked? I had no idea. But it was bad. It was never to happen again. And we should never talk about it.

And we never did.

Chapter 2

Innocence

Heaven knows I tried.

Every boy was in flag football. It was all anyone on the play-ground could talk about. I was an inch or two taller than the average third grader, which destined me to be a receiver. My featured play was "wide left"; get off the line, go three yards downfield, then dart left to the sideline for the catch. Otherwise, I was to stay and block. After practicing for a month, we finally got a chance to run the play in an actual game. "Wide right" was the command from the side-lines. I blocked. The same play was called four times with my coach and teammates becoming increasingly exasperated at my seeming unwillingness to move off the line. Wide right. I blocked. It turned out I was to go downfield whether wide left or wide right was called. But coach had learned his lesson and never called either play for the rest of the year, sealing my reputation as physically incompetent.

I was also a sad excuse for a Cub Scout. The Pinewood Derby was the event of the year—you might remember the drill. Every kid was given a block of wood, and a kit with axels and wheels. Your task was to saw, sand, and fashion your car into a lean, aerodynamic model of an Indy 500 speedster. Each Scout would then load their replica onto an inclined track, invoke the spirit of Al Unser or Mario Andretti, and let fly. The facsimile that went the fastest and farthest won. The trick was not just carving your wood into something sleek and aerodynamic; it also required an ability to grease the axels and carefully position metal weights beneath the chassis.

As in many suburban competitions, it was probably more about the adults than the kids. Boys would come in with tricked out mini-Porsches, clad in jet black or cherry red epoxy paint, perfectly weighted, with graphite treated wheels that seemed to spin on their own. It really called for planning, a circular saw, and a father. But my dad did not know how to be a dad, and I think it was just too painful for him to learn. I had sandpaper, some left over bright orange hazard paint, and a fear of noise, engines, and sharp surfaces.

It was not so much losing that was upsetting, it was losing so badly, and the grim certainty that I never had a chance.

Everyone knew but me.

The kids started calling me faggot, pussy, and sick. I had no idea what those terms meant other than I was acting "girly." It seemed to have something to do with the way I spoke and the way I carried myself, natural behaviors I could not have changed to save my soul. It also had to do with physical awkwardness and my admittedly timid, non-confrontational nature. School-aged boys run in packs, the pecking order is strictly enforced, and I was near the bottom. It is my hope than no kid ever grows up in a world as homophobic as Simsbury in 1972. I did not even know what homosexuality meant, but I knew that being a "fag" was the worst possible insult. Interestingly, kids that were horrible to me on the playground were often much kinder when they were not running in the pack. I would ask them why they called me fag, and they would tell me I acted like a girl. In what way? You just do. And I would have to leave it at that. But it haunted me. When I complained about it to my parents, dad just said "Punch them in the nose, or they will think you are a coward." And I was.

One spring my class did a project on filmmaking. My role was to be the thief fleeing the scene of the crime, only to be shot by heroic cops. Around this time there was a syndicated show on TV called *Thrillseeker* featuring clips of wiry acrobats and other amazing athletes performing daring parkour-like physical stunts while in the background a driving soundtrack played an exhilarating tune that went something like "da da da da, da da da da, da da da da, da da da, Thrillseeker!" When I got fatally shot in the film, I indulged myself in a prolonged elaborate death scene, first falling to my knees, one hand clasped to my breast, the other trembling in front until I slowly, dramatically surrendered to the earth.

I thought I was the next Brando. But my peers howled. They wanted me to fling myself violently onto the ground as if I been exploded by a grenade, which risked undesired physical harm while preventing me from displaying my full thespic talents. The whole class started calling me "Thrillseeker" and wherever I appeared on the playground I would hear kids in the background singing "Da da da da, da da da da, da da da da, da da da da ... Thrillseeker!" then laughing uproariously.

I loathed being teased and having paper clips and erasers launched at me from across the room. I despised myself for not fighting back, one against the playground. I was at the top of my class academically, but started skipping school, complaining of stomach-aches, just to avoid the other kids. I erected a basketball hoop and spent countless hours shooting on my own, so at least I knew how to dribble, pass, and make a lay-up, anything not to be the scapegoat for a month. I would have traded every single "A" I ever got for just once hitting the home run or being the boy other boys wanted to be around.

Thank God for summers. I loved swimming and exploring and there were so many glorious weeks when all I had to do was read wonderful books like *Treasure Island*, *Johnny Tremain*, *The Phantom Tollbooth*, and my all-time favorite, *My Side of the Mountain.* The latter classic was written by Jean Craighead George about Sam Gribley, a boy my age who decides to run away from the city to a rugged, secluded area in the Catskills where he can fend for himself while extending his scientific knowledge of plants and algae. He also finds and tames a peregrine falcon, Frightful, who becomes his friend and companion. It combined all the things I loved: science, nature, and a brave boy my age who lives by himself and does not have to contend with bullies.

I adored the book, and one afternoon I got a chance to watch the Canadian movie adaptation. Everything about the movie entranced me and I can hear the mostly cheerful, but at times haunting score in my head anytime I want. Teddy Eccles plays Sam in the film. I knew he was beautiful, although I did not understand what that meant at the time. I would have done anything to be his friend, for I was so lonely once I closed the book.

Life was confusing enough. Getting older just made it worse.

At the end of fifth grade, we got the "boys talk" which I found equal parts creepy and hilarious, since it involved a variety of physical and emotional experiences too ridiculous to conceive much less describe. Like most kids, I found the concept that I was created by my parents having sex ludicrous and slightly horrifying. My humiliating experience with David taught me the first and most important lessons about sex, that it had something to do with your privates and that it was dangerous and never discussed openly. Nudity was gross. Sex was nasty and not a topic of discussion amongst decent people. Neither of my parents ever mentioned anything about it, although I was gifted a modest book called *Growing Up* with a few anodyne diagrams and a picture of two naked preschoolers. It was clinical, condescending, and raised a lot more questions than it answered. However, much to my horror I found myself daydreaming about naked kids, boys and girls, and what they looked like. Hair started growing in places where I would prefer it not to, and acne appeared overnight.

Right around this time I discovered that my father and I had more in common than I realized.

I may have been outwardly "good" but that did not alter the fact that I was both sneaky, and when motivated, artful. There were no secrets from me in that house. On afternoon I found Dad had a stack of *Playboy* and *Penthouse* magazines hidden in his bedroom closet on the far left, carelessly concealed under some dress shirts. Any young man armed with pluck, motivation and a desk chair could surmount that obstacle.

As much as anything, I just wanted to learn about this mysterious world everyone referred to, but no one discussed. It was illuminating. First, my father had a secret sexual life that he hid, and in the room he shared with my mother no less. And the girls were beautiful. Once the door had been locked and double barred, it was just Miss

July and me. They were not dirty, more like the girl who served you cotton candy at the county fair, but lots prettier ... and naked. I was eleven. I did not know how to masturbate. I just rubbed my jeans until my penis hurt. In some ways it was vaguely comforting. I was so scared of everything, but these girls (and they were usually in their late teens or early twenties) loved animals, walking on the beach at sunset, and baking cookies for their boyfriend. It was like having a babysitter with benefits. Mostly I discovered it was normal for men to have a secret life that you never told anyone about which involved nudity and other things alluded to vaguely in the hideous "boys talk." It showed you were a real man. I spent a long time just looking. No matter how difficult my day was or how mean the bullies were, Barbi Benton would be there at the end, looking sweetly just at me without judgement or obligation, offering everything and nothing.

In fifth grade I finally made a best friend, Terry Wilcox. He would be my constant companion throughout the next three years, and he made those years bearable. He was not as nerdy as I was, but close. And now that I had an ally we did everything together; building forts, having sleep-overs, and watching *The Brady Bunch*. Terry's parents even took me with them on a road trip to his grandmother's in Virginia. Sitting in the back seat I read Richard Adams's *Watership Down*, and we all sang along to Van McCoy and the Soul City Symphony's *The Hustle* whenever it played on their little Chevy's AM radio. I had my first Dr. Pepper (a revelation since it was still a regional drink) and went sailing on Lake Jefferson. I loved being included in a group.

In 1972, my father got tickets for the UConn-Yale football game played down in New Haven at hoary and then-decrepit Yale Bowl. This was a huge deal for me. I followed the Cleveland sports teams religiously. It was my one "guy" thing. Maybe I did not have intrinsic athletic ability, but that did not keep me from rabid fandom. No one else in my family cared. My father and I went to three sports events in my life, Navy-Michigan football in first grade, Connecticut-Yale as above, and a Hartford Whalers hockey game in junior high. They were big deals, and I recall each contest vividly.

Dad invited Terry to come along with Sue and Richard Carlson, our next-door neighbors. The Carlsons were kind people. Mrs. Carlson worked as a secretary for an insurance company in Hartford. The office received a lot of mail from exotic places such as New Zealand and Austria and she would save the stamps. I collected everything, especially stamps, so the highlight of my week was visiting her on Friday afternoons to see what discoveries she had found for me. I was thrilled they were joining us for the trip.

We all piled into our banana-colored Pontiac station wagon, the Carlsons in the back, and Terry and I in the folding seats in the rear. We rarely went on an outing. I was so excited. On the way down we drove past the Connecticut Reform School for Boys in Meriden. I could imagine no worse fate than being locked up in a school where all the other kids were bullies. I never wanted to be a bad boy and end up there.

We chatted merrily for a while before I heard my dad proclaim to all assembled in an unmistakably loud voice "I had been a little worried about Jimmy, but he has been stealing my *Playboys* so maybe he will turn out okay after all." I was mortified, but I knew who that message was for, and as humiliating as it was, I also felt a tiny sliver of pride at having pleased my father. I remember nothing about the actual game.

The fall went well after the Yale fiasco. Last place in the Pinewood Derby, but first place in the Science Fair (a lovely diorama of local birds and flowers). Terry and I were tight. Even the Browns were good; they went 10-4 that year and came close to upsetting the undefeated Miami Dolphins. We were leading 14-3 at the half but ran out of steam. Not the last time the Browns would break my heart.

I hung out at the coolest place in town for a fifth grader, the spanking new West Farms Mall. Anchored by W.T. Grants and an A&P, it was the most recent sign of progress in the form of suburban sprawl. My haunt of choice was the Paperback Booksmith. Normally I would go looking for nature books and sometimes history or sports. One day as I was making my way back to the nature guides, I passed a photo book by David Hamilton, *Sisters*. Most people do not recall Mr. Hamilton, which is probably just as well. In the early 70s, he was notorious for soft core photography of very young girls. That stuff was more available in stores than it is now. Plus, it was not really porn, it was erotica, art!

My memory of the cover was of two young girls in very gauzy clothing, as they were about to kiss. Everything was hazy, like the lens was dipped in Vaseline before shooting. The back of the book showed more images. Hugh Hefner loved well-endowed women. These girls were petite, almost boyish, not fully matured, and you could see their developing breasts behind the thin layer of linen that served as a pretense for clothing. The book was wrapped in cellophane, so I could not see the treasures within, but I was dying to see more.

At eleven, I was a dirty young man. And I was obsessed. Somehow these photos were more exciting and arousing than anything in *Playboy*, even if they did not show as much. But I would never in a million years have the courage to do what I so wanted, which was to buy the book. It was nasty. I was nasty. And I knew the rule: never let the world know how nasty you are.

That book haunted my days and nights. The girls were only a few years older than I was, but they would not make fun of me or humiliate me, which was my eternal, over-riding fear. They had something that I wanted, needed. I kept going back, making sure no one saw what I coveted. But that infuriating cellophane prevented access to all the treasures hidden within.

One day I just could not stand it anymore. I cased the joint. Where was the staff, when was it quiet, where could I crouch concealed? It was November, so I could wear my capacious blue winter jacket, too big, but I would grow into it. I carefully moved the book to the part of the rack farthest from the counter and brazenly slipped *Sisters* under my jacket, clutching it with my right hand. I was shaking, terrified, but managed to stroll out of the store without suspicion. For days, every police siren was sure evidence that the case had been cracked and I was headed to juvie.

I should have learned two lessons that day.

First, anticipation surpasses possession. The book was not all that. The girls were cute, but not as cute as fantasy promised. On the ride back, balancing my bike on busy, twisty West Mountain Road with my left hand, while supporting the book with my right had been thrilling, but once the plastic wrapper was off, reality turned out, after a few minutes of painful rubbing, to be underwhelming.

And then the waves of shame, guilt, and remorse. I stole a book worth three months of allowance. I had brazenly trashed the Eighth Commandment. If I were caught by either my parents or the police, I would and should go to the dreaded Reform School in Meriden. And I would have to admit to my mother than I was going to jail because I had stolen a book with pictures of naked girls. I might have chosen death over disappointing my family like that. After just a few days, overwhelmed with guilt and fear, I grabbed the book from its hiding place under my mattress and righteously tossed it into the municipal trash, where I could not easily retrieve it. I was ashamed I had stolen it, but relieved and a little proud to have gotten away with it, knowing I would never ever do it again, at least not until next time.

The second lesson I wish I had figured out at the time was that sexual desire is transformative in potentially dangerous ways. I was no saint, and I wanted things. I doubt *Sisters* was the first thing I ever stole. I imagine I had purloined a pack of gum or a candy bar or two; little boys do those things. But *Sisters* was larceny on a whole other scale. This behavior was totally out of habit for me. I was a "wimpy little pussy"; everyone said so. But erotic desire transformed me like spinach transformed Popeye. It gave me the strength of a thousand men, and yes, a certain thrilling power. At eleven, I was destined to become a sex addict.

Although I was obsessed by my little world, the rest of the country was engrossed by Watergate. Over the previous year or two our family had abandoned the communal kitchen table to have dinner in the living room. The evening ritual demanded the local news at 5:30 and the CBS Evening News with Walter Cronkite at 6:00. For my family, particularly Dad, it was an hour that documented the steady erosion of all that was good in America. I would not say he hated blacks, but he hated civil rights. If blacks stayed in their place, and stayed respectful, he was fine, happy to shake their hand. But when they started wanting things beyond their level of understanding or competency, it infuriated him. He happily left Cleveland, which had transformed into error and corruption when it became the first metropolitan area to elect a black man as mayor (Carl Stokes in 1967).

The Vietnam War, which seemed to go so well for so long, angered him as well. I knew we were winning because every week the casualties for the primitive Viet Cong were described as five to fifteen times the casualty rate for Americans. At that rate, in a year or two there would be no North Vietnamese left. But dad thought the liberals were forcing our military to fight the war with one arm tied behind its back; we should just nuke the whole place and get it over with. Environmental wackos were destroying business by equating yellow-bellied marmots with human beings. Women's liberation and the Equal Rights Amendment were disgusting and unnatural. Fags and hippies were omnipresent and entitled. The outrages of the modern liberal world were legion and inexorable.

Dad was also drinking more. Like seemingly every other suburban WASP family, the liquor cabinet was an important fixture in our home. The top surface was finished in gleaming copper. There was plenty of drawers for exotic instruments like muddlers, jiggers, and strainers. Inside the cabinet were rows of bottles, like a line of exotic dignitaries. The bottles were from all over and reminded me of stamps with their antique labels in foreign languages. The smells were intriguing even if they burned my nostrils. Over time I learned that most of the bottles were for show. Dad was a vodka man. It was the sovereign remedy for the stress of a long workday. The first shot or two mellowed him out, but by the end of Walter Cronkite, the fallen, corrupt nature of the world was laid bare. Mom tried to calm him, and gently push back on his more violent opinions, but a man's home is his castle, and he was God-damned if he was not going to say exactly how he felt in his own living room.

Although my father possessed a universal dislike for almost everything that was transforming a world dominated by men that looked and thought like him, his special contempt was reserved for hippies and fags. He hated long hair, disrespect, and disobedience.

The '60s were not a decade of progressive change, they were a constant assault on everything he believed made America the greatest country on Earth. Nothing galled him more than stories on Stonewall and gay liberation. Gays were always portrayed on TV as hyperfeminine, garish, drug-addicted sex fiends destined to go from one anonymous pick-up to another until they died alone, probably from some horrible venereal disease, understandably hated and shunned. He once told me if I ever smoked weed, he would break my arm. But I knew that for Dad there were worse things than smoking weed. And I realized in some still undefined way that when Dad was yelling at how much he hated all the degenerates on TV, he was warning me.

Yet, for all the raging at the TV—("McGovern, you miserable goddamn son of a bitch ...”), by 8:00 he was asleep, and the next day it was as if it had never happened. He was never like this in public. No matter how angry he got, he never raised a hand to me, ever. But I realized there were two sets of rules: in public we followed the explicit rules, be nice to everyone, have Christian values, accept the nature of change. But it was all a cover; once at home, watching *All in The Family*, he was Archie and Archie was the hero, and Meathead was well ... Meathead. Your private self and your public self were separate. It was important to present a certain exterior to the outer world, but it was a guise to permit you to interact with a morally decadent, rapidly deteriorating society. Only at home can you feel good about being the decent white heterosexual male God made you. Everyone else was jealous; screw them. And if anyone at home could not play by these simple rules, screw you.

The summer before I entered sixth grade, our family spent a week vacationing at the Chautauqua Institute on the lake in western New York. It was like a summer camp for families. We went to shows, played shuffleboard and rode around on bikes. It was a rare time free from television, an intentional nod to simpler days, although I do remember Nixon's visit to China being announced in the communal dining hall, since it was such an important story.

Chautauqua is a glacial finger lake seventeen miles long but only two miles wide. An old-fashioned ferry connected the two sides.

We had distant relatives staying directly across from us on the opposite shore and one day we crossed the ferry to visit them. The family had two children: Jack, who was my age, and his sister who was maybe two years older. It was the summer I had cut my big toe, which was covered in a large, bulky ace bandage. To my chagrin, I could not go swimming. We messed around a bit and played croquet where I was singularly focused on maneuvering my mallet while chary of my injured toe.

Excitedly Jack said "My sister has a secret. Wait until you see what I found." We sneaked into her room, where he showed me a copy of *Tiger Beat*, or a similar magazine for young adolescent girls. He pointed out an image of a 12-year-old boy from Quebec named Julien Trevoir, who was becoming a popular young singer. The caption read "Girls, Ooh-La-La!" The picture was of a soft, almost androgynous looking boy sporting a Prince Caspian page boy haircut with a mysterious, sweet, but somehow beguiling smile. His shirt was unbuttoned several inches down his soft unmuscled chest. I was smitten, my heart started thumping, the rest of the world faded away. It was just me and a picture of the most beautiful boy I had ever seen. Jack thought it was hysterical that his sister loved this magazine. If he only knew.

I kept sneaking back to his sister's room and that magazine. Jack finally caught on, and asked "What is wrong with you? You are even weirder than my sister."

I remember nothing else. I could not stop staring. I had been excited by pornography, but this was thrilling in an even more powerful way. For one thing he was about my age. We could be friends, maybe even best friends. As a pop singer, he must lead a glamorous and exciting life. I could not stop looking at the picture. I could sense he knew something special, something great to say to just me, alone.

If we were best friends, nobody would tease us, because he was famous, and the girls loved him. He could have the girls if I could just have him. The picture was more sweet than sexy—the latter would have freaked me out—but he was pretty and intoxicating, and I wondered what he would look like with his shirt completely off. I loved that he was French-Canadian, it made him even more exotic and exciting. He was clearly still a child like me; there was not yet anything repulsively adult about him. We could have adventures just like the ones on the Partridge Family or Brady Bunch.

Finally, I had to let the magazine go, and have never seen it since, although I hunted it for years. The drive home was a nightmare. Dad was drunk, and the ferry was closed by the time we left. So we had to navigate a thirty-mile drive through dark serpentine roads to reach a location we could see from where we started. Dad was tired and pissed off. I amused my younger brothers while my mother pleaded with him not to get us all killed. Miraculously we made it home in one piece, my mom using it as an opportunity to warn us against drinking too heavily. Another teachable moment squandered.

That one photo of an angelic boy triggered an obsessional, yet comforting world that I still intermittently inhabit. It was the beginning of a complex secret life. Like most kids, I spent a great deal of my time lost in daydreams, often about unobtainable athletic or social success. We all want to be the hero. I did not fit in at school, and it was clear that the authentic me was not welcome at home. So I spent hours dreaming about being in a band with Julien. He became my go-to preoccupation for any idle moment.

That world adapted over time as does the music I think we want to play. Neither of us are twelve in my imagined world, although that is the age we meet. I often fantasize myself as adopted, and Julien and the band became my virtual family. I dream of our blossoming career, traveling from city to city, becoming famous together, but the fame never interferes with our relationship. There is almost no sexual component to these thoughts, which I think is odd, since mutual desire is always simmering in the background. The dream focuses on doing something important in life and being recognized for it.

I have spent thousands of hours in this alternative reality. For the many years I lived alone it nurtured a safe place to be myself, to construct what an ideal life might look like, at least to the young adolescent part of me that had to disappear within myself to survive. How much of this secret world is my own developmental immaturity and how much is familiar to others in uncertain to me. I believe that many of us have a private inner life, but I only know mine.

I knew I was different long before I knew why I was different. I did not connect with my younger brothers through no fault of their own. They were authentically interested in normal stuff like GI Joes and roughhousing on the playground. They did not have my peculiar terror of being "bad," and easily made friends. That left me lost in a hazy secret world of my own, which I was terrified to share with anyone.

I did have a glimpse now and then that I was not as alone as I thought. There were two other boys in school who were perhaps even more fabulous than me –, Billy Bingham and John Mason. John was quiet, gentle, and the most clearly effeminate boy in our class. He looked and dressed as a boy, but his mannerisms were precise, delicate, and rounded somehow. I caught myself glancing at him many times for confusing reasons. Billy was the live wire of the duo. In his basement was an elaborate and extremely detailed scale model of Disney World, which had just opened in Florida. He would spend hours constructing dioramas of cool rides like Pirates of the Caribbean and Space Mountain. Like me, he avoided physical confrontations, although I did not know he took private gymnastic lessons. The day in gym class when he revealed his skills on the uneven bars by performing spins, twirls, and leaps that the other boys, even the jocks, could only dream of, still stands in my mind as a miraculous revelation. In hindsight he was the coolest of us all. Billy and John were even more ostracized than I was but had the superpower of just not giving a fuck. They had each other and felt no desire or pressure to move outside the world they created for themselves. I did not have the strength to join them; it would have meant surrendering my pantomime of normalcy, and I was not ready for that. I was lost in a world of "Don't ask, don't tell."

One afternoon, tired of watching me mope around, dad told me in vodka-induced candor "Jim, stop feeling so God-damn sorry for yourself. Why can't you realize that you are the luckiest kid in the world; a smart, healthy, white American boy who doesn't realize everything is being handed to you. Anyone else would kill for your life!"

Dad loved me, and he believed what he said. I had it a lot easier than he did growing up. I just needed to follow some simple rules, and if I did, he was certain the good life would flow effortlessly in my fortunate direction.

He was right about it all of course.

I wish I could have told him that acting normal is like holding your breath underwater. It is not as easy as it looks.

And you can do it for only so long.

Chapter 3

Preparing to Fly

The best thing about childhood is reliable progress. We get bigger, stronger, smarter. Privileges accumulate, and even in dark moments we can be certain tomorrow will not look like today.

I moved from Tootin' Hills to Henry James Junior High where my primary concerns on the first day all focused on my locker. How to find it, unlock it, and most importantly, how not to get stuffed in it. The previous summer, Terry had moved to Buffalo, which was sad, but I was not completely isolated. As a seventh grader I started to form alliances with others who were socially maladroit. We were still teased mercilessly by the bullies, but we were at least teased together.

I spent most of my spare time solitarily shooting hoops and reading, then re-reading J.R.R Tolkien's *Lord of the Rings*. Tolkien's Middle-Earth was another fantasy world to withdraw into when this world seemed unbearable. I would still purloin Dad's magazines but also cut out pictures of boys from *National Geographic.* I vividly recall one of a shirtless Australian kid cradling an injured bird in his arms. Why did I find boys my age or younger so alluring? I prayed it was a stage everyone went through that I just needed to outgrow. I hid the picture behind homework assignments posted on my bulletin board but would pull it out so I could stare at him as I compulsively rocked to the radio ("WDRC—the Big D—Hartford. Stay tuned for Casey Kasem's American Top 40!"). I always had a rocking chair and the swaying rhythms pressed deep grooves into the carpet of my bedroom. At almost sixty, I still calm myself by rocking on a pillow while listening to music.

I thought about Julien all the time. That summer he was a guest star on an ABC variety show hosted by Howard Cosell (!), but the songs he sang were forgettable lightweight fluff. In some ways the less information I had, the easier it was to idealize and objectify him into something safe and appealing. Mom casually "reminded" me that summer that if any of her boys turned out to be gay, it would mean she failed as a mother. Just in case I forgot.

I relished the school part of school. Mr. Smuckler, my seventh grade biology teacher wore a Marines buzz cut but he let me and my chums play paper football on the lab bench as long as we kept our grades up. History and English were easy and fun. On the other hand, gym was a nightmare. Being around other semi-clothed guys was both thrilling and terrifying. I loathed my awkward, pimple-laden body, and could barely look in the mirror, which meant I wore the same pair of jeans and ugly W.T. Grant generic striped shirt daily. For my money, I could have gone toe to toe with The Elephant Man for body of the year.

I was resolute that no one would see me in my underwear, so I wore my gym clothes under my jeans and assiduously avoided the showers to hide my shortcomings. I could tolerate basketball—all those hours of shooting hoops by myself paid off—but in general I dreaded the gymnasium. Dance was coed and the girls cut lines to avoid being paired with me. But wrestling was the worst. I was terrified of touching the boys, some of whom were quite pretty. What if I got an erection? People would know and the universe would cease to exist. Sexual humiliation always felt like a heartbeat away. I endured until school was over and I fantasized that the school bus was our band's tour bus, and behind me was not some kid flinging paper footballs at me, it's Julien, in a blue silk shirt and a crimson scarf, like Fred in *Scooby-Doo* giving me a soft reassuring glance that reassures me he will keep our secrets safe.

I attempted life on life's terms but found it wanting. Joe Cohen was in my homeroom, and we became acquainted. He was not my typical friend; he was handsome with long, black hair and a quick, sarcastic wit. He was also an athlete. I had no idea what he saw in me. We started hanging out after school, and he tried to teach me tennis. Being his friend seemed very important to me, and I saved up to get a new racket (it was not good to be seen with mom's Alice Marble model), and practiced my serve by hitting against a wall for hours at a time. Muscle memory works even for me, and I started getting better. I loved being the friend of a cool kid, particularly a handsome one like Joe. I wanted to be around him, and I would do almost anything for the opportunity. Occasionally a crazy thought would come into my head that I might want to kiss him. When I had those thoughts, I would just purge them through reverie and my rocking chair. Joe and I were spending so much time together the other kids started to notice. We had done a science project together that I thought was quite cool, but out of the blue, with no warning he yelled at me that I had ruined it, and then he destroyed it, very publicly so that all the other kids could see. "Peak and Cohen are getting a divorce."

The last thing we did together was play an atypically vicious game of tennis which he won 6-0, 6-1, so I guess he got a chance to assert his dominance. Only now can I see it may have been as much about his fear of being attracted to me as it was the other way around. Tragically, it was probably the closest I ever got to a same sex-relationship. I just did not have the courage to swim against the tide of my family and the world. That was madness, and somehow, despite a daily flood of confusing lustful thoughts, I still clung on to the mirage that I could make rational choices, that my brain was my friend and only wanted the best for me.

It saddens me to know that people want to restrict LGBTQ- related books from public schools and libraries because of a fear children can be lured or brainwashed into "choosing" deviance. That is a grave misunderstanding of human nature. It is so much safer and easier to stay with the herd. There is an old proverb that states: "the nail that sticks up will be pounded down." I knew that. Kids have always known that. Those of us born with atypical or simply broken systems of orientation or gender need guidance, not silence. Postponing difficult conversations because it makes adults uncomfortable only confuses and discourages teenagers and renders them prematurely cynical.

I tried joining things, but I was not much of an asset. Another nerdy bespectacled young man named Glenn talked me into joining DeMolay, which was essentially junior Masons. It involved a lot of silly pseudo-religious rituals and secret handshakes. The ritualized meetings where the officers were supposed to inspire us to live "clean, manly, upright patriotic lives which will be a credit to our families and friends" usually ended in farce since no one remembered their lines. Even if they did, they were unable to utter them with a straight face. I think the only reason they let me join was, like Larry Kroger in *Animal House*, they needed the dues. The crowning event of my DeMolay career was when the group drove up to Riverside Amusement Park in Agawam, Massachusetts on a summer night before eighth grade. They forgot to bring me home, and I waited past midnight for my parents to come get me. The only other social activity I participated in was confirmation in the Methodist Church, where the other kids sipped wine on the sly and passed gas every time the Pastor mentioned Jesus. In my emotionally self-absorbed world, I really needed God, but He seemed distant and mocking at best, illusory at worst.

So, I studied, three to four hours a night. It was one thing, maybe the only thing, I could do and do well at that age. And I knew there were other worlds out there, worlds beyond junior high, beyond Simsbury. College could get me out of this trap, and I plotted escape.

Obsessed with uncomfortable sexual thoughts, often involving kids my age or younger, knowing that interacting with actual human beings was anathema, I spent a lot of time skulking around bookstores and the public library. All it took was an interesting scene or two to make a book worthwhile. I discovered quite a bit of homoeroticism in classics like Twain's *A Connecticut Yankee in King Arthur's Court* where in the final scene our hero is enclosed in Merlin's cave with "52 fresh, bright, well educated, clean minded young British boys." Later Twain notes "they were a darling fifty-two, as pretty as girls too."

I also would have been very willing to go to sea with the

welkin-eyed "handsome sailor" who is the center of Melville's *Billy Budd.* Innocent and beautiful, Budd murders his ship's master at arms in a fit of passion and is sentenced to death by the ship's captain Vere, even though Vere knew the evil Claggett had pushed Billy to the fatal act. Vere's assertion that "at the last Assizes it will acquit," that God would pardon Budd, even if his fellow men were unable to, gave me hope that someday He might understand my struggles. I still was not fully cognizant how far off the beam I was. I knew I liked young boys more than I should, more than was helpful, but I figured as I got older, the people I was attracted to would get older with me, and that somehow I would get used to girls.

Another mild catastrophe occurred after my sophomore year. My father, ever restless, had earned his law degree and found a new job working for a tennis ball felt manufacturer in upstate New York. The summer before my junior year we moved from suburban Hartford to suburban Albany. I missed Connecticut but was grateful for a chance to make a fresh start socially.

I intuited that I needed to change if I wanted to be happier. I always felt not being athletic or part of a team handicapped me socially, which inspired me to share how alien and inept I felt with my health teacher. Mr. Vanover was a rookie teacher, a young, animated man with a shock of chaotic auburn hair, an omnipresent track jacket, and an unnerving tendency to say "Yeah baby" when happy, and "Holy mother of pearl" when things were less sanguine. For reasons I could not fathom, Coach V felt I was deserving of his time and energy and recruited me to be on his indoor track team. I suppose I must have presented a challenge; if you could coach me, you could coach anyone. What I lacked in speed and strength I compensated for with abysmal technique. My innate gait is less of a dynamic, propulsive stride and more of a minimalist zombie-esque shuffle. I can hear him now: "Jeeesus, Peak—Holy mother of pearl—molasses runs faster."

I might have been the least talented runner in Bethlehem Central High School's long and storied history. But Vanover never quit on me, even though I could do nothing to help his team. He had me run through drifts on snow days to improve thigh strength. He talked to me about nutrition, and the importance of upper body strength for a good glide. He told me how to meditate and center so I could be fully focused on the task at hand. I made real friends for a change, and felt part of something bigger, something real. We sang school fight songs on the bus to meets. I got invited by other kids to dinner. It was the first time I belonged.

And I got better. Instead of being worn out after walking the track, I discovered I could do my patented Peak shuffle for miles and miles. I was slow, but I knew I was improving, and even dreamed of finishing in the top ten, and earning a point for the team. Our first meet was at the old Albany Armory. I was entered in the longest event, four miles, which was sixty laps on the tiny gym track. It was my first competition since my star-crossed days in flag football. The starting gun went off, and I fell behind. Coach screamed at me, hair flailing like Gene Wilder's in a hurricane; "Peak, don't let 24 out of your sight." V was trying to monitor six guys at once, and I was fading fast, but he refused to ignore me; he was resolute lap after lap. "Peak, be the fly in his ointment, Holy mother of pearl, run, run, run!" After three miles my chest was aflame, I could barely breathe, but still I was passed by the better runners, and everyone was a better runner. I was finally on the last lap when I realized I was the only one left on the track, running it solo, struck by the futility of my efforts. The Niskayuna coach yelled "Why don't you get off the track, the girls have sprints to run" and I considered following his suggestion when Coach V suddenly materialized by me side, agitated and animated, "Finish, finish, finish strong." I somehow sprinted to the end, legs shaking, wanting to vomit. Last place, but I had given it everything I had, and refused to quit. Coach V came up to me, put his arm around me, and said quietly, "Yeah baby."

I was never a good runner, but I got better, and could generally finish within distance of the guy in front of me. My indoor track varsity letter is more precious than my diploma. As lousy a runner as I was, Coach V made me feel as important as any kid on that team, and in difficult situations I can hear him in the background imploring "Holy mother of pearl Peak, compete, compete!"

But I only had two years in Albany, and it seemed just as I was finding my stride it was time to leave. I had taken every challenging course I could find, read voraciously, and had no social life to distract me besides track. SATs and Achievement Tests were right in my wheelhouse; doing well on them came naturally.

And here I shockingly was able to bring a small bit of glory to the Peak name. I was neither handsome nor athletic, and certainly not very masculine, but I was bright and determined, and like my father, I craved the external validation that I could make it, and be somebody. Going to a prestigious selective school was an imprimatur of potential, particularly in my striving WASP culture. It was my way of leaving years of social torment in the dust. For my family, climbing the social ladder was corroboration of their drive and validated the huge financial sacrifices required to put three boys through four years of private school. I know it was a tremendous symbol of their love and confidence, and their belief in our potential. I can never be too grateful for that loving gift.

So I applied to the most prestigious small school I could find, and ended up at Williams College, only a hundred miles from home. My acceptance made Dad so proud, it was the boast of every cocktail party for a year. Not even the boss's son could get in, which tickled him to death. The kid who recruited me for DeMolay in Simsbury applied and was rejected, which made me secretly rejoice.

Maybe I was better at this life thing than I thought. Maybe I could fake it after all.

Chapter 4

Williams

I spent the summer before college working nights loading Coca-Cola trucks. The work was hard but paid well ($8 with overtime!). It provided a contrast between the working-class life I thought I was too good for, and the pure life of the mind I envisioned commencing in September.

Williamstown is a sublimely beautiful college town in the far northwest corner of Massachusetts. It is also an outpost of elite power and privilege; a "Little Ivy." Looking good was important to my family, and important to me. Socially I was swimming in a much deeper ocean. My classmates included a boy whose father was a member of President Carter's cabinet, the daughter of Vincent Price, and for a brief period, the son of the Shah of Iran.

On the first day of freshman orientation, my dad drove me to Morgan Hall in "the Banana Boat," our ancient sickly yellow faux-walnut veneered Ford station wagon. After unloading my belongings, Dad and I celebrated my coming of age by journeying north to Vermont where the taxes were lower, and the vodka cheaper. In 1980, eighteen was the legal age and I purchased my first alcohol. A true naïf, I somehow settled on the combination of Southern Comfort and Mr. Boston's blackberry brandy (which I thought would be a pleasant fruit flavored spritzer). Poor choices individually and repulsive when combined. Even more intriguing was the presence of an adult bookstore just over the state line (zoning laws were less restrictive in Vermont than in Massachusetts), a novel sight and duly noted.

Overnight I knew people from Manhattan and the toniest suburbs of Boston and Washington, D.C. They owned summer homes on Martha's Vineyard and spent Christmas skiing at Gstaad. At times it appeared everyone was blond and drove a Saab. It was snobby, but I wanted snobby. Not to belittle others, although I was not above that, so much as to avoid being belittled myself. No one goes to these schools because they learn more there. A motivated kid with access to a decent library could learn anywhere. It is all about validation. When you go to Williams you are anointed to the elite. That is why every kid applies to these schools, and why parents cheat, lie, and bribe to get their kids in.

Academically, it was heaven. Reading *Ulysses* with the foremost Joyce scholar of the era. Taking art history and discovering Botticelli and Vermeer. For Intro to Computer Programming, the class had access to a UNIVAC computer the size of a city block. You did not write the program on the computer directly, instead you typed punch cards, which were then fed into the mainframe. One Friday night I mistakenly wrote a program with an infinitely repeating loop. My professor told me running it all weekend consumed $10,000 worth of electricity before he manually terminated it.

I was no longer the only person who did the homework. Yeah, those kids were rich, but they were also smart, confident, and driven. I overestimated my abilities and enrolled in an advanced calculus class which retrospectively I had no business taking. It was designed for the kids who would design operating systems and open hedge funds a few years later. The final was so theoretical it might have been written in Sumerian. I escaped with my first C.

My social deficits remained, but I gamely tried to work through them. Like so many socially anxious people, I thought I unconsciously emitted a pulse wave of desperation that "cool kids" instinctively recognized and avoided. But although Williams was chockablock with confident, socially superior beings, there were enough freshman like myself that I could find safety in numbers.

My roommate Alex was the brilliant son of a Greek émigré, focused on fast cars and quantum mechanics. I never studied in my room because our suite was Alex's realm and he was constitutionally incapable of completing his problem sets for physics without ear shredding heavy metal (his Holy Trinity consisted of Pink Floyd, Jimi Hendrix, and Led Zep). He loved designer jean jackets and sported an awesome euro-fro that would have made Bob Ross jealous. He wore his family wealth quite gently, but not many twenty-year-olds drive turbo charged BMWs. Physically he embodied a certain restless energy, seemingly everywhere at once. Last I heard he was chairman of an artificial intelligence lab at Cal Tech.

During freshman orientation we had co-ed seminars where we discussed the environment, equality of the sexes, and what George Orwell's 1984 portended for society (we were *the* Class of 1984 after all). But once the men retreated to their half of the dorm the conversation coarsened. Alex and I had as much familiarity with women as penguins had with sunburn, but along with the rest of the guys we talked a good game.

Before Facebook there were "face books." At Williams it was called the "Class Book," and it consisted of head shots of each incoming student along with their name, hometown, and high school. No textbook ever received as much loving attention in college as the Class Book; mine was in tatters by the end of the semester. Initially you were just trying to memorize the names of your 499 other classmates, but the guys, especially after a beer or five, used it to rate the "hotness" of our female peers. We also noted which men were handsome, with the pretense of acknowledging the competition.

Williams was a fabulously pretentious place, dangerous for someone whose identity was the consistency of wet cement. The college admissions process had taken up most of the space in my brain for the last two years of high school, which allowed me to postpone social concerns. Now that the dog had caught the truck, he was not quite sure what to do with it

My hazy sexual restlessness was unfocused but insistent. The men and women of the Class Book were universally well scrubbed and attractive, but I lacked a certain intensity.

One night Alex said "Peak, look at this poster, there is a daquiri party over at the Berkshire Quad. Let's go talk to some girls. I don't want to go alone."

"I'm not sure man," I replied. "What is a daquiri anyway? (I pronounced it as "Duh-quir-ee"). Isn't Berkshire an upper-class dorm? Senior women don't want to talk to us."

"It's pronounced dah-quir-ee Peak, dah-quir-ee. And by the looks of you, you could use about four of them. Mars needs women, let's go."

Together we went on patrol. I obtained a Solo cup of cold red slush smelling vaguely of strawberries and airline fuel. We assumed a position on the periphery of the activity, where there were fifty people flitting in and out of the dim, fluorescent outdoor lighting. *Purple Rain* throbbed in the background. After twenty minutes or so of us gazing at our sneakers, Alex saw his chance when a small opening between several coeds presented itself ten yards away. "Wish me luck. I'm going in." I was the wingman, left on the sidelines. The drink was foul, I but swallowed it quickly and got another.

All I could think was well, here I am. Now what?

How did these people get the courage to talk with each other, when they are all strangers? I alternated between feeling invisible and painfully conspicuous and isolated.

In many ways college was everything I dreamed. I loved discussions and lectures, found interesting people to talk with over lunch, and made friends in class and at the dorm. I learned to DJ and hosted my own college radio show on WCFM. But introduce even a possibility of intimacy into a situation and I froze.

What did women want?

I could no longer say it was looks. My acne was gone, I wore contacts, and could at least pass for human at this point.

What was wrong with me? Why did actual adult relationships give me the creeps? Personal cowardice was my all-purpose go-to excuse, but it was self-deception. I am tough in my own way. My "problem" at eighteen was that I was still artless and innocent enough to feel uncomfortable with the public projection of a false self. Sadly, I would develop this skill over time.

In October I finally followed my heart and hiked the three miles up US 7 to visit the "adult store," praying that no one would see me.

The store smelled of sweat and desperation, like the poorly venti-lated locker room of a losing team. The light, like the atmosphere, was sour yellow. Just two sections: magazines and paperback books. Videos did not yet exist.

I had never seen anything like it. It went far beyond *Playboy* or the most exotic magazine my dad picked up from trips overseas. The magazines were graphic and to the point. No Stephen King short stories or NFL previews here. There were magazines for fe-tishes I knew, and several I had no idea existed. *Huge Tits, Poppin' Mamas* (pregnant women), and *Cherry Tarts* (eighteen-year-olds dressed up as adolescents with short skirts and pigtails). Depravity of every description. The familiar combination of simultaneous arousal and disgust, otherwise known as the Jim Peak special, in all its glory. I could not even look at the magazines. They were not just graphic, they were too much, so fake, so sad, women as meat. Turning away was not so hard for me.

Then I went to the books. Again, every fetish, but just words, no pictures, somehow less personal, and less distressing. And I could find themes that turned me on, like *Teacher Loves Her Students* or *Hot Aunt*. For the first time I purchased porn, bought it with no eye contact with the clerk, who had no need for eye contact with me. There is no boredom quite as profound as the boredom of the adult store clerk. I scurried back to school, double locked the door, masturbated, and then, in my age-old pattern, threw them away in horror.

I thought of what my dad had said, that I was the luckiest kid in the world, but only if I played by the rules. If I didn't I would lose everything. I must figure out how to fall in love and have sex with a woman. How difficult could it be?

In freshman orientation I noticed a petite blond from Georgia, with a honeyed accent and a boyish bob, who seemed interested in me. Courtney had been raised in a very conservative Christian home; Williams turned out to be her parents' worst nightmare. She left the South a good church girl and came back an ardent un-repentant liberal feminist. One afternoon I asked if she wanted to go with me on a hike up Pine Cobble, a little hill overlooking campus. "Darlin' I thought you'd never ask" was the unexpected response. I think it was the first time I ever asked a girl to do anything.

It was almost too beautiful to be real up there, encircled by the Berkshires and the Green Mountains, every hillside painted with the electric display of reds, yellows, and oranges that is uniquely New England. I was so happy to be here, and happy to be with Courtney. She was great to talk to, for once she had escaped the clutches of her evangelical upbringing she was like a horse let out of the barn. We discussed politics, the existence (or lack thereof) of God, and whether Flannery O'Connor or Eudora Welty was the better writer. I enjoyed being with her. She was a friend, and gave me an opportunity to feel normal.

I saw her on and off all fall, but never felt an urgency to press it farther. I liked her, and she was cute, but not what I dreamed of at night.

When I casually mentioned her to my parents at thanksgiving break, Mom picked up on it instantly. "Jim, that is so exciting. I was wondering when we were going to finally hear about a nice girl. What are her parents like? Any brothers or sisters? Are you going to get her a little Christmas present?" "Mom, she is just a girl, I just thought you would want to know." "Well, if that girl has any brains, she will be talking to her parents about what a nice boy she met this fall at school. We are close by; tell her she can come visit anytime."

Of course, by this time I was learning to play the game myself. It made me happy to make my parents happy, and nothing made them happier than hearing about a nice girl. The best part of Christmas break was not presents but the reruns of *James at 15*, a TV show starring a young and handsome Lance Kerwin. In my favorite episode Kerwin's character awkwardly but charmingly loses his virginity to a Swedish exchange student. If Lance could do it, so could I.

One frigid, snowy winter night in January I attended a mixed drinking party. Courtney was there.

How does one make a pass? That was the question I was asking myself, but really the better question should have been how does one fake desire? I wanted to be like everyone else. I wanted to see the elephant and not feel like the most incompetent man in the world.

A long January night of drinking ensued; I remember feeling so warm from the alcohol. Between Courtney and me lay an almost empty bottle of tequila. Playfully she turned to me and said, "Jim, if you eat the worm, you will be my hero." Fair enough. After doing her bidding, I felt I had earned a right to a request of my own slurring out the words "I want to have sex with you." Not surprisingly the response was a gentle, but firm "Sweetie, who are we kidding, go to sleep." I have darkness in my nature but not dark enough to confuse the meaning of "no" and decamped to my spinning bed as confused and confounded as ever, with an extra dose of humiliation on the side.

I was too embarrassed to say much after that. Courtney continued to want intellectual conversation about Foucault and the nature of reality but not much else, at least not from me. And of course, in a way I was quite relieved, not having to have to go through with something I really did not want to go through with.

I noticed flyers for the Williams Gay and Lesbian Alliance. It included an anonymous phone contact to learn how to attend meetings. I saw it, was interested in it, but did not have the moral courage or honesty to act. I was not sure I was gay. I liked Julien, but not men.

But I sure was not straight, which was horrifying. Unforgiveable really.

I was terrified of being excluded from the warm cocoon of privilege and incapable of looking directly into the mirror of my authentic self. If the adult me had one thing to say to the younger me, it would have been, go to the meeting, and try just once to be a vulnerable, transparent person. It was a missed opportunity.

The school year ended uneventfully. After a lackluster first semester, I figured out how to study more effectively, and more importantly how to avoid calculus. I had made a drunken, stupid pass at a girl I respected and was firmly and appropriately rebuffed. Back to rocking on my bed while dreaming about a smash appearance on *American Bandstand*.

Freshman year was about to end, but home and Albany did not

beckon. I had to find a summer job that would provide a little money, but would not be too unpleasant, and preferably, outdoors, tired as I was of the confining New England winter. Williams had a great career counseling center with a small section on locating summer jobs. My first choice was to go to Yellowstone and work in the park. But although I mailed out an application in January I never heard back. The job coordinator suggested working as a camp counselor. It would not pay a lot ($800 for the summer), but room and board were included, and it looked to be easy. I signed on and found a job at Camp Bucktail, a fancy, expensive place right on a beautiful spring-fed lake in the Berkshires, where I would help guide a cabin of twelve-year-old boys. I thought it would be pleasant enough.

We spent about a month cleaning the camp up. It boasted amazing sports facilities (clay tennis courts, just like at the French Open!), and an interesting, diverse staff. The camp aggressively recruited English college students who looked at the opportunity as a kind of paid vacation while providing the camp a certain overseas cachet. We had a splendid time, working outside in the day, drinking beer at night.

Finally, in late June, the campers arrived. They were generally wealthy East Coast Jewish kids whose families had sent their boys to this camp for generations. I co-counseled with Richards, an education major from Sheffield who bemoaned the fact we called football soccer while dourly noting American beer was pale goat piss compared to a genuine English stout. We made a great team.

One day, Richards and I were assigned to watch the littlest kids, six-year-olds. We went snipe hunting, inventing the characteristics of the legendary marvel of the woodland forest as we went along. Look for a yellow underbelly boys, remember he has eyes on stalks six inches high. They like to hide in logs. Sooner or later, all the kids excitedly thought they caught a sight of one. They were adorable.

Camp brought out many of my better characteristics. I had never really worked with children before, and found I was a natural. Some of that junior high school nerdiness had finally dissipated, but I very much remembered what it felt like to be sad or lonely or confused, and I recognized it in the kids I was responsible for. I think they in turn felt safe around me. The camp was expensive but very well run, with lots of support and supervision. It also allowed me to be back in the woods, and there were lots of opportunities to go camping and hiking. I liked the kids, they liked me, it seemed swell.

In the middle of the summer was the most crucial, pressure filled event of the entire season: Parents' Day. Everyone and everything had to look good. It was the only time counselors were expected to accompany their charges to the showers to make sure the little barbarians emerged looking and smelling human. So, I took my group of sixth graders in. The showers were communal with room for about twenty.

Everyone stripped down. Remarkably, this was just about the first time I had seen actual boys naked since being "caught" with David twelve years earlier. When I was in grade school I went on several sleepovers and caught a glimpse or two of Terry, but it made little impression at that age. In middle school, death would have been preferrable to showering, and since it was not required, it did not happen.

But in that shower, I finally got it. Irreversibly, terminally got it.

I saw those naked glistening bodies and my throat went dry. The room wobbled. I had no idea they were so beautiful. The small penises and buttocks, water cascading down their chests and legs. They were laughing and joking and having fun, but all I could do was look. The extent of my guilty arousal left me breathless. I grabbed my towel and fled.

That night I left Richards in charge and went over to the vacant tennis court, climbed up on a rock and sobbed. Just sobbed. My yearnings were not a temporary phase; they were my shattered reality. This is how I am supposed to feel around women, or at least adults. But I felt it around twelve-year-old boys. I knew they were cute, but everyone thinks they are cute. I had desire; desire that made no sense, a desire that was perverse and contemptible. But there it was. This was the thrill that motivates a boy to kiss a girl, risking rejection and embarrassment. I thought I just did not possess it. But I did possess it, in spades, but for the wrong people. And it was not a phase I was going to outgrow. There was no mistaking what I felt.

Stupid brain.

Because I loved the picture of a pubescent Julien, I feared being gay, but now I realized that I should be so lucky.

It made no sense to me. I knew there were despicable child molesters out there, who I presumed were wicked, evil people who hurt children for the sheer joy of doing so. I loved children, the last thing I wanted to do was hurt them. But I desired them and coveted their bodies. I was not just a freak. I was an abomination.

The night was beautiful, full moon, light breeze, a symphony of crickets and cicadas. But it was no longer Eden for me. I had been summarily expelled from the garden, and blasphemed God from one side of the Milky Way to the other.

That rest of that summer, I debated my unpalatable options.

I could kill myself, but that was weak and cowardly, and life was good in many other ways. The truly awful thing was that I could tell no one, ever. There was no way to explain this. I was a deviant. No one would or could understand, much less help. And if my family found out, it would destroy them.

With hindsight I can track how my sexual map became smaller, more specific, and less adaptive all through high school and college. I did like the girls in *Penthouse* but now registered that even in junior high I always liked the more petite, the more boyish, the youngest-appearing girls. Smaller breasts were more attractive than the large busts my friends coveted. Plus, it took nudity to get me to really notice women. I knew that some women are more attractive than others. I knew some men were more attractive than others, but no adult is so attractive that I gave them much more than a second look. But twelve-year-old boys. I always noticed boys. Always. It is not something I planned or plotted. It just happened.

I struggled the rest of that summer with coming to grips with my tangible reality.

Self-loathing became second nature. I loved the kids. I also loved looking at the kids, and I hated myself for that love.

On the last night of camp, I had made special treats, and made an honest but overwrought speech about how much I would miss them. They liked me, but they did not love me as I loved them. They loved their parents and were excited about going home after a summer in the woods. But I was immature and emotionally needy and tried to make them feel guilty about not being as sad at parting as I was. I wanted emotional reciprocity from them, ludicrous as it sounds. Love makes you believe strange things.

I feel shame about inflicting my emotional neediness on those boys, but over time have developed some sympathy for my twenty-year-old self. I was an alien in a dark place, with unspeakable fears, terribly alone.

Chapter 5

Encased in Concrete

My camp experience had been terrifying. I was a pedophile, a word so revolting I could not allow myself to invoke it even in thought. I had no idea what to do, other than hide. Some people come out of the closet. My plan was to enter one, encase it in forty tons of concrete, and have it dropped by a trawler into the Marianas Trench.

Distraction and denial were so much easier back in Williamstown. No little kids wandering around, so my moral deformity was easier to ignore. I could just focus on my studies. Shockingly, although never the center of attention, I found myself surrounded by friends, and my pervasive sense of seeming "odd" and inadequate slowly seeped sway. For my male classmates, I fabricated an elaborate story where I had sex with multiple European female counselors from our sister camp to cover up my hapless virginity. Implausible as it was, they bought it. Just like my parents did. Life lesson: never underestimate how much people prefer an appealing lie to an unpleasant truth.

At twenty I did not anticipate the catch. Get too good at playing a role and you begin to fool yourself, not just everybody else. Breaking faith with your authentic self is a bitter price to pay for a conventional life. Any sexual minority can attest to this.

I loved English classes, especially the Romantic poets. To be twenty reading Keats and Shelley for the first time is emotionally and intellectually transporting. They were passionate young men intoxicated by an optimistic vision of the Enlightenment. Their poetry celebrated a world of freedom and equality and inspired a hope in universal justice and peace. Their contemporary, Wordsworth, documented the everyday ecstasy of the natural world, consolations always available to me in Williamstown, with its ever-beckoning hills, woods, and streams.

Although not talented in the field, I admired the logic and precision of chemistry. But I adored English, so I majored in both. While studying, I would periodically become restless and would comb Sawyer Library looking for something of prurient interest. In the photography section there were bound volumes of popular magazines like *Camera Today* dating back decades, which I hoped might contain a candid picture or two. One evening I stumbled upon an advertisement for a book entitled *The Boy: A Photographic Essay*, published by a company called Book Adventures in the mid-1960s. The advertisement included several samples of "innocent" art photos of naked young boys in casual poses. Of course, I was instantaneously aroused. I combed the stacks for similar ads. But every time I found another issue I discovered that all the pictures had been carefully removed with a razor blade. It was the first time I surmised that I was not the only one with a secret shame.

I spent one summer back at Bucktail. They loved me there. It was an uneventful season. No drama this time. I knew what to expect, and had better emotional boundaries, which resulted in a more positive experience for all involved. The next summer I worked at a local bank and relaxed. I still stalked bookstores, always searching for the perfect picture. Amazingly, I found an actual copy of *The Boy* at The Question Mark Bookstore in Albany, but was too embarrassed to buy it. The following day I screwed up my courage and went back the shop, but it was already gone, never to be seen again.

I went back to the things I did well which looked good. I applied to medical school. The advantages were several. First, both the application process and then school itself were all-encompassing activities, easily crowding out internal conflict and confusion. And I genuinely like people and like helping. Medicine was a stable, honorable profession which would make my family proud. I applied to a dozen schools and was admitted to several. I desperately wanted to follow several of my friends who went to NYU, but tuition was well over $20,000, far beyond my limited resources. Instead, I attended a public institution, Upstate Medical School at Syracuse. Initially I felt sorry for myself that I was stuck in snowy upstate New York instead of living the high life in Manhattan. But those four years in medical school where the happiest of my life.

In late August 1988 I steered the "Banana Boat" west towards Syracuse and dumped my few belongings in front of Weiskotten Hall. My classmates were no longer the sons of the American Ambassador to the Court of St. James, or heirs to a real estate empire; instead, these were the sons and daughters of postmen, barbers, and teachers. They were every bit as smart as I was and often worked harder than I did. Many were older and had practical life experience.

Lucas was my first roommate. He entered medical school after serving in the Navy as a surgical tech. He was cynical of civilian ways and deployed a dour little smirk when amused. He presented as calm and unemotional, but behind the military demeanor was a complicated man with his own secret issues. I once chanced upon his hidden pictures of shirtless young men and knew he was in the closet, but we never discussed it. We talked about his Detroit Tigers and my Cleveland Indians, upcoming exams, where to train after Syracuse. Don't ask, don't tell was convenient for us both. We could have helped each other, but layers of shame obscured any possibility of transparency. I was married when he finally admitted he was gay, after having been dishonorably discharged from the Navy for an affair with an enlisted man. At the time I did not have the courage or transparency to share that my struggles were even darker than his.

Those first few weeks were tough. I was drowning in the information deluge, and failing three out of four classes, wondering how I was going to explain being kicked out of medical school to my mom. One afternoon I had slumped onto a sofa in our small TV lounge, intending to indulge in a brief, solitary pity party when a beautiful, curly-haired woman with gorgeous soft brown eyes and a broad welcoming smile asked my name. "Jim Peak" came the monotone reply. At the time I was calculating how many years I would have to work in the seasonal department at KMart to repay my loans.

"Jim Peak! That sounds like Jiminy Peak." (Jiminy Peak was the name of a humble local ski hill.) "Yes," I replied, "and you ..." "I'm Frannie, from Scarsdale." From an inauspicious start appeared one of the best things in my life.

Fran was the child of two Iranian (they would say Persian) physicians who fled their country in the late 1950s to find asylum and medical training first in Canada, and later, in the U.S. I can only imagine difficult it must have been for Fran's mother. To successfully become a female physician in Tehran would be daunting on its own; subsequently starting a new life thousands of miles away sounds overwhelming. Tragically, she had poor command of English, struggled to pass the licensing exams, and was therefore unable to find employment as a pediatrician. This left her socially isolated, financially dependent on her husband, and at times, embittered about the loss of the professional role she had worked so hard for. Her husband, Raj, was more fluent and would become a renowned professor of pathology at the New York Medical College in Westchester County. They had five children, three of whom became physicians themselves. I am not sure any alternative occupations were considered, much less encouraged.

Fran is funny, warm, and endlessly supportive, with a wicked sense of humor and a sharp nose for gossip. We would spend all Friday and Saturday night studying, finally dragging ourselves back to the dorm at midnight. I would stop by a convenience store on the way home, buy a four pack of Bartles and Jaymes (wine coolers were the hard seltzer of the era) and we would decamp to the basement of Clark Hall to mindlessly watch *Beavis and Butthead* on MTV. After an hour or two I would put my head in her lap and she would sweetly stroke my hair. There was nothing sexual between us, just a warm sustaining friendship. Fran has a deep yet simple connection to the Spirit, while my connection always seems wobbly, inconsistent, and ephemeral. She is the ground wire. The ancient elm tree on the village green providing shade and comfort to all.

Fran and I became close friends with Joseph, the pampered only son of a wealthy Jewish ophthalmologist in town. Instead of residing in our modest student dorm, he had his own luxury high rise apartment overlooking the rest of the city. He drove a new Volvo and wore Armani sweaters and bowties. He never allowed us to forget that he was a Cornell graduate, but at heart was a sweet, decent guy who took our relentless ribbing in good stride.

Growing up, the only gay role models I knew were the Village People. Medical school shattered those stereotypes. Victor was one of my partners in anatomy lab. He was a Manhattan native, and a cultured older man who had attended Princeton and the Yale School of Drama. Always dapper ("nylon, ugh, only natural fibers caress this skin") and well groomed, he had a quip for everyone and everything. He had friends in film and on-stage and knew "Meryl" from back in her waitressing days. Victor was tall with an erect carriage, arresting blue eyes, and a receding hairline that was the bane of his existence. He was campy, wicked, and comfortable in his own skin, which my family told me would be impossible for a gay man, who should be haunted by self-loathing.

Whenever an unexpected assignment appeared, he would cock his head, give me a sideways glance and whisper, "Kill me now." Incoming male first years were noted with the pleased murmur of "Bless my thighs, fresh supplies." However, you only had to be with him for a few minutes to realize the campy persona was just an amusing act, and that he was a deep and serious guy behind the wisecracks and the cashmere scarfs.

He was open about sex and desire in a honest mature way that felt light years ahead of my peers at Williams. "Snookums, it is Saturday night. I have studied for twelve hours. I need to get laid." He had known he was gay since junior high school; his family was utterly accepting, and his openness a revelation. He loved opera, Broadway, and Armisted Maupin's *Tales of the City* series, which he loaned me, and I voraciously consumed, both because the stories were as addictive as a box of chocolates and because they opened a parallel world of gay culture I was simultaneously drawn to and frightened by.

These were my new and wonderful friends. It has become almost cliché to reassure young LGBTQ kids that "It gets better." But it does. Your tribe, your group, your family is out there, as desperate to find you as you are desperate to find them. Never stop looking.

Nothing drowns out the background noise of broken sexuality like spending forty hours a week cutting up dead bodies. My cadaver was the first corpse I had ever seen.

Everything about that class was a struggle for me, particularly the vast amounts of memorization—bones, muscles, ligaments, arteries, nerves, and veins, many of which had obscure Greek and Latin names which all sounded alike. You did not want to confuse your gluteus maximus with your extensor carpi radialis; otherwise, you would not know you ass from your elbow. (Sorry, I couldn't resist.) I might have been able to visualize two dimensional spaces without much problem, but adding a third taxed my limited working memory, like imaginary numbers did back in calculus. I could memorize the branches of the radial artery or the origin and insertion of the masseter muscle; but knowing what was dorsolateral to the anterior head of the pancreas required an almost insurmountable barrier for someone who did not figure out how to tie his shoelaces until third grade. (Thank you, Velcro!)

Our first formal test was based on the dissection of the chest. I studied hard and thought I was ready for the exam, which featured videotapes of partially dissected cadavers. The examiner would point to a very specific anatomical feature, and we had to select the best of five options. How hard could it be? The correct answer was "Harder than you could ever imagine." Every muscle, every nerve and blood vessel all looked the same shade of lumpen grey; half the time I did not even know what three of the five responses referred to. I thought I was a diligent student, but I realized I needed to find a whole different gear of academic dedication if I was going to survive.

Grades were posted after every exam on the "wailing wall" outside the classroom in the gloomy basement of Weiskotten Hall. We gathered as a team. Lucas smirked that it had been a basic exam, and he hoped it would get more challenging in the future. About three fourths of the way down the roster was a red line at seventy percent; everyone below it was at risk of failure and having to repeat the entire year. I made the mistake of scanning for my student ID number from the top down. It would have been quicker to begin at the bottom and work my way up. I was about the fifth number below the dreaded red line with a 68. Fran had a 63. Joseph had passed with a 75 and put his arms around Fran and me, happily remarking "I love your guys; you are my buffer." After the grades were posted most of the class went to a local park to celebrate, but I walked disconsolately along the empty streets of Syracuse dreaming about Julien and wondering if I could open a record store if medicine did not pan out.

I never studied so hard in my life as I did that first semester. Most days Fran and I took a late afternoon break to stroll around Oakwood Cemetery, designed by Frederick Law Olmstead of Central Park fame. The only other respite was on Wednesday evenings where everyone yielded to the escape of intramural volleyball. Victor invariably wore a t-shirt that warned: "Age and treachery will always overcome youth and skill." Otherwise, it was cram sessions at the library or at Sutter's Mill, an infamous college dive bar at night but a quiet med school hangout during the day. I gained ten pounds that fall, mostly from their glorious French fries drenched in gravy. One restless night I dreamed Rufus T., the name we had given our cadaver, was posing me questions based on his own corpse, sadly disappointed by my ignorance, which implied a poor appreciation of his corporeal sacrifice.

Finally mid-December arrived, and with it the anatomy final. By this date I was just above the dreaded red line on the class list on the wailing wall, but a summer spent repeating anatomy sounded dreadful. Fran and I studied on the top floor of Weiskotten one last time the night before the final exam. The myriad branches of the facial nerve were bedeviling me. I had one of the worst colds of my life. At midnight the custodian showed up and reminded us the only reason we were up so late was that we had chosen to wait until the last minute to study. Miraculously both Fran and I passed, not by much, but passed. I have never been so relieved in my life.

I spent most of Christmas break in bed, while being treated for pneumonia, tired but happy.

In my first year we only had one afternoon a week where we were allowed to work with actual patients. The long-tailed coats we wore in anatomy were filthy and redolent of formaldehyde, but for Intro to Patient Care we finally were allowed to wear our short white coats. The instructor, Dr. Voyich, reviewed the basics of taking a brief history and interviewed a pleasant lady with bronchitis, who left with a script for amoxicillin and an inhaler. A mantra of medical education is "See one, do one, teach one." We had seen, now it was time to do, and our preceptor had one last patient in clinic. I expected someone like my Grandfather Root complaining of an irritable stomach or lumbago. So I was surprised to see Dr. Voyich enter the room accompanied by a tremulous young woman with large brown eyes wearing a modest white dress. Her name was Maria, and she had just turned eighteen. She looked like a nervous little bird. I felt awkward for her. Victor would have warned me that no gentle thought goes unpunished.

Our instructor pointed at me; "Mr. Peak, start us out with some basic questions about the chief complaint and associated symptoms." No, Lord no, not me. I knew nothing about anything. Alas, there was no escape. We stammered to each other like two junior high students at their first dance. "So, um, I am MS1 Peak, thanks for coming, I mean being here, so what might be bringing you to our little clinic today?"

"Oh, Dr. Peak, I hope you can help me. For the last four days I have felt so dizzy and tired. I feel like I always want to throw up, and (here she blushed coyly and averted her gaze a bit) I have been having some cramping "down there." Finally (here she looked away completely) my nipples seem so tender and painful. I am scared. What's wrong with me?"

Oh no! Even a student as inexperienced as I knew the basic symptoms of early pregnancy. She seemed so young and so distressed. My first patient. Do I skip to a diagnosis or ask what she was doing last Friday night? What exactly is the appropriate follow-up question to the complaint of tender nipples? I desperately glanced at

Victor who silently mouthed "pray for death" before looking the other way. My cheeks flushed stop sign crimson when I attempted to inquire whether she had experienced "um, any romantic interactions which, might have possibly, or not, possibly, involved some manner of physical congress, of a perhaps intimate nature, uh more precisely intercourse with, um, anyone, recently, last week or two really, ah, um, anyone?"

A deep, profound silence pervaded the room.

Maria's eyes widen. Oh no! Dr. Peak, you can't possibly think I'm pregnant."

I looked at the ground and stammered on. "Possibilities, nothing definite, certain criteria would have to have been fulfilled. Hopefully a good thing, or not. Really not for me to say."

"Doctor, oh no!"

I shot a pleading glance towards Dr. Voyich.

He just smiled beatifically at my precocious young patient, and said "Maria, great job, we so appreciate the theatre students volunteering their time to teach our first years."

Maria gave me a little wink before exiting stage right. Thus commenced my clinical career.

Chapter 6

An Interlude of Snowfall

Once I was convinced I would not flunk out, medical school transformed into an exciting, happy experience. Although I knew almost everyone, Fran, Joseph, and Victor were my closest friends and we generally studied together. Shared suffering bonded us together like basic training comrades. It was us versus the faculty and a relentless exam schedule. We secretly loved the intensity of the work even if we kvetched along the way.

Victor and I were the only two left in the pathology lab one grey January afternoon. We were becoming more and more friendly, although he always carried an air of mystery about him. I had heard hints about a boyfriend back in Manhattan, but gathered that time and distance had inflicted a toll on their relationship, and he had been uncharacteristically gloomy of late.

Upstate New York is infamous for its sudden and dramatic lake effect snowstorms. When we entered the lab at noon there was a lazy flake or two flitting down. By the time we left at 5:30 there was four feet of snow, and no sign of stopping. Victor gazed out into the sea of white and sighed "I needed this like a third penis. Fortunately, Snookums, we are close to the only decent Pork Lo Mein in town. After culinary reinforcement we hazard the maelstrom."

We had never done anything together, just the two of us, and although I could never match his repartee, I was obviously good at playing a straight man.

He once told me he considered "upstate" to be everything farther than a ten-minute taxi ride from Lincoln Center. So, what was a nice Jewish boy like him doing in the frozen tundra off Lake Ontario?

The story was fascinating. Not surprisingly, finding an acting job after Yale was easier said than done, so he found himself moonlighting at a Bellevue Hospital dermatology clinic during a pivotal time in the late 80s. Almost overnight the clinic had become overwhelmed with previously healthy young men presenting with Kaposi's sarcoma, a rare skin cancer usually only seen in older men of Mediterranean descent. Many of them also had odd lung infections typical of immunosuppressed patients on chemotherapy. And they were virtually all gay men. AIDS had made a dramatic, indelible impression on the city's medical community and Victor was swept along in the tide of mystery and tragedy, quickly becoming an expert on early recognition of Kaposi's. But he wanted to do more than diagnose; he wanted to be part of the cure. This led him to medical school and Syracuse (or as he referred to it, "Siberiaberg").

The storm finally died down after dinner, but both of us were tired of neuroanatomy so we trudged to his apartment where we drank gin and watched a campy old horror film involving female vampires (or as Victor called them "vampettes") who for whatever reason always lost their blouses just before plunging their fangs into the tender flesh of innocent young men.

I was puzzled, but Victor solemnly informed me "All vampettes know you can only drink an Adonis's blood if topless."

So many things I did not know. I was happy and relaxed.

Next thing I know Victor's hand is stroking my thigh.

Somewhere in the depths of my brain, an alarm went off: "Pass warning." I never knew that alarm existed, since there had been no previous necessity. Another theory launched from the dim recesses—"He must think you are gay, isn't that funny."

Thoughts began to cascade in every direction, like a bucket of ping pong balls thrown down an apartment stairwell. "Why would he think I am gay? Just because we like all the same things. And why would he I think I like him, just because he is funny, kind, and sweet." Then some more dangerous ideas crept in. "You made a half-hearted pass at Courtney, and were rebuffed, why would it be so bad to half-heartedly accept a pass from someone you are more emotionally attuned to."

Furious replies flew out from the more primitive cortex. "I can't be gay, what would people think. Plus, who are you kidding, creep. He is a man, hair everywhere. Gross. That is not what you want. I know you too well. You like him, but you don't want him. You want Julien, or someone like him, but you can't have either. You can't have anyone. It is just as well you are not attracted to Victor, because you do not deserve him. You are a living, breathing boo-by-trap. Don't destroy him with you."

I murmured "I am sorry Victor, but it is late, and I have to get up tomorrow and study," before commencing the dark lonely walk back home, escorted by a gentle but heavy and steady snowfall, erasing my footsteps.

Chapter 7

Among Patients

After two long years in the bowels of Weiskotten Hall we were finally unleashed onto the wards of University Hospital as newly minted third years. We had five major rotations that lasted 6-12 weeks each: medicine, surgery, pediatrics, psychiatry, and ob-gyn. I certainly thought about entering pediatrics, given camp and the fact that I enjoyed kids. At 23, I knew I was attracted to children, but I was very aware that was wrong, and I was committed to not hurting kids. I noticed attractive patients. I think most physicians have some level of physical attraction to patients, but it is not too hard to repress that in a clinical setting. Hospitals are not sexy places in general. Spending excessive time looking at growth and development pictures in the pediatrics textbook was about the creepiest thing I did in medical school.

Surprisingly, pediatrics was not my favorite clinic. There were a lot of babies and while everyone including me, loves babies, giving them shots and examining their howling little bodies is unpleasant. I loathed drawing blood and IVs, which requires a professionally detached demeanor even if the kid is shrieking and sobbing. Plus, in my limited pediatrics experience, the children were either very healthy and did not really need to see the doctor or very sick with cancer or cystic fibrosis, which was unbearable to witness. We had several kids die while on the service. I attended the autopsies. Pediatrics was not for me.

Psychiatry made me much happier. I like stories. I like people. I am keenly aware that existence is fraught with snares, obstacles, and paradoxes. I fully understand that most people cannot bear looking directly at the glare of their inner contradictions, and just want to get through one more day. The existential despair of recognizing that life is finite and free will is mostly an illusion seems to be most helpfully understood in communion with another sharing the same fate. The most powerful thing any healer in any profession can do is listen and try to understand.

For all its faults, inadequacies, internal contradictions, and despised status, psychiatry is still the field of medicine that understands this truth the best, and as such it is the most human and maybe the most sacred field of medicine. I admire courage, which is required to see any mental health professional for the first time. No one enjoys acknowledging a lack of control over thoughts or emotions. But the most stable of us, indeed the strongest of us, are never more than a millimeter away from catastrophe. We are all vulnerable. The mentally ill just have a more acute knowledge of this universal truth. Helping them walk with it is extraordinarily difficult and draining; it is also the best job in the world. I have a mental illness. I treat mental illness. Both roles have much to teach.

Grades in medical school were much simpler than in college: honors, pass, conditional, and fail. I had been an indifferent student the first two years, most of which were spent memorizing vast amounts of technical knowledge in pathology, anatomy, and physiology. I worked hard just to pass everything, and never was at the top of my class. But clinical settings required a different set of skills that corresponded nicely with those in my personal toolbox. I genuinely enjoy talking with people and found I had a knack for making patients feel comfortable. I had been so awkward for so long, but through sheer repetition, had learned to feel increasingly comfortable in professional settings, and I started getting honors grades in tough rotations, and began to feel a hard-won confidence in my abilities.

But troubling sexual thoughts were never far away, particularly on weekend nights. Sometimes I felt like that drama student, pretending to be someone I was not, trying to fool the audience.

Sometimes girls would flirt with me for a minute or two, but my anxiety and ambivalence extinguished even random sparks. I did ask one of my female classmates once why it was difficult to find someone to date. She knew me well, lowered her gaze and brutally leveled with me: "Jim, you know you have no sexual threat." Never request the truth, you might get it.

At least I had my dirty bookstores. There were five in the city, and I knew each one. Though terrified I would meet a professor, patient, or student in there, lust overcame fear. I loved leafing through the books.

My favorite stores were ones that resold smut from the 60s, such as the Liverpool Press. When I found a group of books that had what I wanted, time stood still. I went from book to book and became expert at flipping through them, looking for the watchwords that indicated I was in the right place such as "teen," "budding," and "hairless." I would spend forty minutes on my haunches at the lowest level of a bookrack obsessively pouring over every book. I just wanted to remain in the hazy world of hopeful anticipation, where sexual nirvana was always just a page away. Eventually I would tire, go home, masturbate, and finally drift to sleep listening to The Smiths.

Over time I would accumulate a little hoard. I did not care about plot. I only wanted a description of the forbidden. But the more I read, the more I started to write my own books in my head. At first this was hard for me, as I had good internal inhibitions about fantasizing sexually about children. If it was the work of another, that seemed to distress me less, but over time, the more I read, the more it did not seem quite so horrible. Other people had the same thoughts, they were just thoughts, you cannot hurt ink and paper after all. So, I slowly allowed myself to fantasize, first about pubertal girls, and then, powerfully, but more guiltily, about pubertal boys. Somehow the homosexual "sin" was almost more shaming than the underage theme. But it remained my secret world, and I rationalized I possessed an impenetrable mental wall which sealed my inner life against the external world. That was error, but when you are walking an unmarked trail it is easy to lose your way.

The four years of medical school passed too quickly. Before I could practice independently as a psychiatrist, I would need to spend at least another four years as a resident. My dad wanted surgery. I told him that if I became a surgeon no one would be happy with the body count, which he glumly accepted. Unlike college and medical school, where there were always multiple candidates for every empty slot, finding a residency position in psychiatry was easy. I could go pretty much anywhere I wanted. It was a chance to satisfy the wanderlust in me. As a child, I had dreamed of seeing the west coast, so I saved my money and flew off to an interview at the medical school in Portland.

Oregon Health Sciences University (OHSU) is located on Marquam Hill adjacent to downtown. The campus is surrounded by towering evergreens, a contrast from the flat urban decay of Syracuse. At night, the mist came down from the hills and shrouded the entire campus in mystery and peace. The cone of Mount St. Helens and majestic Mt. Hood were visible from almost every corner of the city. The school and the department were top notch. When I was selected for Portland, I was ecstatic.

The question was the same however, whether I was in Connecticut or Calcutta, Portland Maine or Portland Oregon. How to live? I did not want to be a monk. I desperately wanted someone to love and someone to love me. I adored children and dreamed of a passel of them. But my broken brain betrayed me time and time again. People asked why didn't I date? My excuse would be I was just too shy, or I would lie and invent a fantastic sex life from which I was just taking a little break. In college, I could still convince myself that I needed more time to figure out what I wanted and needed from life, or that somehow, I had never met the right person, some - one physically and intellectually attractive enough to thaw me out. Making friends was easy, but making a pass—how did one do that, how did one overcome the terror of a physical connection?

Deep in the darkest recesses of my brain I knew the truth by how easy it was to be excited by a picture of a thirteen-year-old in a swimsuit. That was what made my throat dry, my heart pound, my senses acute. I was never going to get that feeling in a woman. I believed my only path to happiness was through artifice and denial. Like Billy Crystal's Saturday Night Live character Fernando, my family's motto was "It is better to look good than to feel good, baby." Maybe if I just looked good long enough, feeling good might naturally follow. Maybe Holden Caulfield was right, "all adults are phony."

I just needed to check my authentic self at the door and build my life around a plausible act. Doesn't everyone do that to some extent? How bad could it be?

Stupid brain.

Chapter 8

Portland

In June 1988, I followed the advice of Horace Greeley and drove my beat-up Ford Escort westward ho! to Oregon to commence my psychiatry residency and begin again.

I rented a tiny little studio apartment in Beaverton and felt very grown up and lonely. The first year consisted of six months of psychiatry with four months of internal medicine and two months of neurology. Limiting resident workloads to reasonable hours was still a decade into the future so I was spending 80–90 hours a week at the hospital, often going several weeks without a day off.

Initially, I was both exhilarated and overwhelmed with the fact that I was finally performing as a doctor; having my orders taken off the chart and being the first one called when a patient was unstable or when there were questions. Being on call alone was terrifying, but I slowly figured out the lingo and my role in the strange world of the emergency room. All the patients were listed on the "board," next to their age and chief complaint. The chief complaint was usually abbreviated code, like MI for heart attack or "L femur fx" for a broken left leg. Some chief complaints were a bit insensitive, like FDGB ("fall down go boom") or FOG ("friend of the grape," which meant the patient was drunk). My job was to evaluate patients who had a psi symbol next to their name. A psi symbol is a "u" with a vertical line drawn through it and is the universal sign for psychiatry.

The ER is a strange and unpredictable creature. It could be

quiet for days, then suddenly explode into frenzied activity. The multi-tasking was overwhelming; triaging who had to be seen immediately, who required a shot of Haldol for agitation and hallucinations ("Vitamin H in room 3, stat!"), and who just needed time to sleep it off. The crucial task is figuring out who needs to be admitted and who can safely be sent home. There is relentless pressure to keep ER beds open to accommodate new arrivals. I did not have the luxury to be thoughtful and deliberate. I made the best decision I could and moved on.

A common dilemma was the young psychotic person brought in by the police for agitated, confused behavior. Often, they had little insight into their mental illness and just wanted to be left alone. But given the unpredictability of human behavior it was a guess at best. The patients I sent to the psych ward from the ER would be taken care of by the senior residents, which meant their workload was directly related to what I did or did not do in the ER. The best compliment you could get from a senior resident was that you were "a wall," which meant you did not admit very many patients, resulting in a low census and a quiet day. I was a notorious "sieve" because I erred on admitting too many questionable patients, often packing the unit to its limit. I am a worrier. Patients would present with suicidal thoughts, but then would deny them thirty minutes later when they were not allowed to get a cigarette, and I would usually make them stay. It was intense. I remember coming home after being on call 36 hours straight and waking up with my head in a plate full of spaghetti, too exhausted to make it to bed.

One of the first things a young psychiatrist must accept is to not take anything personally or become reactive when patients are angry, threatening, or confused. I like to hear people's stories. I really believe most of us are trying to do the best we can. People who are angry have usually been hurt. People who are full of themselves were often ignored. People who intentionally hurt themselves, or hurt others, usually act out of overwhelming internal pain. That does not mean they made the best possible decision, but they made the best possible decision they could at the time.

Psychiatry was experiencing dramatic change. Eli Lilly had just released Prozac, which revolutionized the field. It used to be that the worst code on the board was "TCA OD" which meant a patient had overdosed on their tricyclic antidepressants. These older medications were sometimes effective for depression but often lethal in an overdose. When those patients came into the ER they were not on the board for long, quickly heading straight to the ICU. Sometimes they lived, sometimes they died.

With Prozac, overdoses were far less dangerous, so clinicians worried less about prescribing them, which translated to a much lower threshold for using antidepressants, often before much talk therapy had occurred. The traditional caricature of the Freudian analyst impassively listening to the neurotic patient on the couch was fading. A new wave of shorter, more practical therapies designed to help patients think more positively and rationally, such as cognitive behavioral therapy, replaced the old approach. These new treatments were designed to provide relief more quickly than the traditional system which was grounded in years of weekly treatment and the intense search for insight. The good news was that severely depressed patients got better quicker. The bad news was that much of human suffering is more complicated than just a little neurotransmitter shuffle. For years I had an old *New Yorker* cartoon taped to my office door which showed a patient on the couch reminding his bearded psychiatrist "Ok, maybe I need to change my life, or maybe you could just tweak my medications."

I did not know a soul when I moved to Portland, but nothing bonds people like proximity and shared trials, and I quickly made friends with my fellow interns. Terry was my first, best friend in Portland. He was yet another openly gay young man. Funny how many gay people there are in the world if you acknowledge their existence, and funny how I was always happiest around them. Terry had been abandoned by his young mother in favor of an oil field roughneck and was raised by his grandmother in an evangelical community near Amarillo. The expectation was that he would marry a fine girl, become a Baptist preacher, and raise a righteous Christian family out on the Texas Panhandle. But God had different plans for Terry. He married said fine girl and was in seminary when he recognized his homosexual attractions in the form of a soft honey-eyed social work student named Brian McKittrick. He made a wrenchingly painful decision to leave his displeased, disbelieving family and together they eloped from the Lone Star state for liberal, wicked Portland where they built a different, but authentic life together.

Terry was a snappy dresser and a touch vain. He possessed a handsome oblong face with grey eyes, an aquiline nose, and a meticulously groomed moustache. The bane of his existence was the wispy thinning hair on his brow. He was always hitting up the Rogaine drug rep for samples. Terry was sensitive, emotional, and extremely attracted to Asian men. After years in the closet, he wanted to make up for lost time. I never knew a man so easily distracted by other men. But he loved Brian, who had stuck with Terry through medical school and followed him to Portland once residency began. Brian was calm, centered, and cowboy handsome. When I first met them, they seemed like the perfect couple, and I got an even more intimate glimpse into a rapidly evolving gay culture. By impulsively fleeing his fiancée for another man, Terry had made a dramatic escape from his preordained life as a pastor, instead plunging head-first into a lifestyle inspired by the campy gay sensibility of movies like *The Ritz*, set in the bathhouse scene of early 1970s New York and *La Cage aux Folles*. He and Brian rented a fashionable little one-bedroom apartment in the Pearl District near the Steel Bridge. I spent many a Friday night there watching moves and eating Thai food. Here were the most out men I had ever known, but I could not replicate their transparency. I enjoyed going to Embers, which had a great drag show. I enjoyed listening to Sister Paula, "America's foremost transgendered evangelist," who had a legendary public access television program in town. I was on the outside looking in, feeling like a platypus, a unique farrago of disparate parts suggestive of many species, but ultimately strange, almost alien.

Work was both challenging and engrossing enough that there was little room for much else, but once I began my third year, I was no longer on call every fourth or fifth night, and suddenly, I had actual periods of free time. Not surprisingly, the freedom was both welcomed and feared. I loved an escape from work, but time off was time to think, and my problems seemed unsolvable. The old desires never abated. After a few months, I had discovered every bookstore in town, and Friday nights were my preferred opportunity to act out. Normal people dated. I, on the other hand, went from adult bookstore to adult bookstore.

Brain and Terry worried about me and my curiously non-existent love life and resolved to find me a woman. It was like a pre-production episode of *Queer Eye for the Straight Guy*. Again, instead of fully acknowledging and accepting the nature of my damaged sexual map I deceived everyone, including myself, with the excuse I had just been so busy working that I had not met the right girl, and that sexual inexperience merely accentuated an inherently reserved nature.

With the encouragement of Brian and Terry, my love gurus, I signed up for a dating service called Great Expectations. Dating services are now passé, but back in the 1980s if you were not comfortable picking up strangers in bars, you looked for something like Great Expectations. Their process included filling out some questionnaires, submitting a few carefully selected photos, and participating in a brief videotaped interview where you would describe what you were looking for in a relationship. It was essentially a more detailed, curated form of the Williams Class Book. You would look at the women's submissions, who in turn would look at yours, and if mutual interest was expressed, a "matchmaker" would set up an informal date, with no subsequent commitment necessary.

I was so deluded. I did not want to date, I just wanted a partner, without the messy, anxiety-provoking rituals which help a couple select for harmonious life goals and sexual compatibility. It was awkward and artificial, and after a few arranged encounters that created no sparks I was beginning to despair.

Then I surprised myself by meeting someone not through Great Expectations, but at work.

Samantha was a cute, intelligent occupational therapist with a bob haircut and warm brown eyes framed by stylish light blue glasses who I worked with in one of the adult units. I had not previously asked anyone out for dinner point blank, but she shocked me by saying yes, and we started casually dating, which I loved. We went to the zoo, and she brought her young nephew along. She had had her own difficult memories of living with an alcoholic father, so we had some things in common and our conversation was easy and pleasant. I liked being seen with a woman. I liked sharing stories, holding hands, and the smell of perfume.

But I knew more was expected and necessary. I had never kissed a woman romantically in my life, but if I could ride a bike, I could kiss. I did not tell Samantha I was a virgin, much less that I had distressing, quixotic desires; that was light years too vulnerable and open. I was not a forty-year-old virgin, but I was a thirty-year-old one, and the role was not as endearing as Steve Carell makes it out.

She made me a delicious fish dinner in her apartment. After cleaning up the plates, I told her I needed a breath of fresh air, which was absolutely true. I walked out into the cool Portland evening and took some deep breaths. This was it. I had read the foreplay chapter of the *Joy of Sex* several times. I had passed anatomy. No more training exercises. Locked and loaded. No turning back. I was going in.

She was in love with me, and I have never been so physically desired before or since. Our passionate French kissing seemed never-ending. Her genuine ardor should have been infectious; instead, it terrified me because I could not come close to matching it. Here was my perfect chance to be normal. A sweet, healthy girl who thought I hung the moon. But as we kissed, all I could think of was any more saliva and I might drown. There were furtive attempts at sex, but I could not maintain an erection. It took me a half second to get an erection to pornography, but in real life, skin to skin, no way. My brain was good at fooling everyone and everything— even itself—but a flaccid penis does not lie.

After a month of internal agony (every time she called my heart dropped and she called multiple times a day) I met her at a café to bail on our one-sided relationship with the lame excuse of "not being ready." She was badly hurt and wanted better, more realistic answers. Her normally soft brown eyes narrowed in fury and disbelief "What do you mean, you are not ready? You are thirty, for God's sake. You are just a child, an emotional coward who cannot make a commitment. Man, your mother must have messed you up but good. No woman will ever be good enough for you." I had nothing to say, since it was partially true, and the full truth was too painful to reveal. Loneliness made me eager to initiate relationships, but once in one, I became terrified of being trapped with sexual demands and expectations I could not satisfy. For someone who told himself how much he hated hurting other people, I seemed to be getting pretty good at it. I was morphing into the boy you did not want to meet. Too bad to be good, too good to enjoy being bad.

Terry and Brian told me I was fine, I just had not found the right one and until I did "just throw that fishy back into the sea." They were being kind, but I knew the problem was not the fish, it was the rod.

Work was my distraction and salve, the one place I felt good about myself. Even now it is so much easier to talk about work than to reflect on my clumsy, inauthentic attempts to forge an emotional relationship.

After several years I finally got the chance to start working with kids, where I was a natural. I saw thousands of patients over about thirty years but remember my first patients vividly, like I saw them yesterday. Chris was a ten-year-old with motor tics who was in foster care in southeast Portland. His mom abused drugs and was unable to care for him. He was anxious and inattentive but essentially sweet and exuberant when happy. His tics were awful, lots of eye blinking and shoulder shrugging. Rather than regular therapy, we would play basketball and talk about how hard it was to wait for his mom to get better, and that it wasn't his fault. He was a great little kid, and I adored him. He once asked me if I would be his dad. That almost killed me.

Our training program was good, and I had lots of supervisors to help with difficult emotions if I was honest with them. I talked to a local TV station about putting Chris on one of their "waiting child" segments, and I think he ended up being adopted by his teacher, but I struggled with the delusion that somehow I was supposed to personally guarantee his future happiness. You cannot keep kids like Chris from their fate, you can only compassionately hear their story and bear witness to the pain.

I learned so much from my patients. Mason was an almost non-verbal fourth grader with autism. I struggled with how to do therapy with a kid that does not talk, but he was friendly and seemed to enjoy coming in. One of my office walls was covered with the artwork of patients, and at one of our sessions I asked him to draw me something. The other kids had drawn conventional depictions of houses and families, but Mason intently and silently spent the next thirty minutes creating a detailed picture of a rectangle with patterns of fantastic dots, spirals, and horizontal lines. I thanked him for his random, abstract art and included it in my collection. Odd kid. A week or so later I gazed at Mason's picture on my door and realized it was a picture *of* my door. Not the usual functional representation of a vertical rectangle with a small off-set circle for the doorknob. Mason had drawn a literal reproduction of what he saw, rows of carefully constructed horizontal lines which mimicked the whorl and spirals of the physical grain of wood. He saw my door for what it was, a complicated unique piece of stained oak, not for its function. We saw the same thing very differently, but his vision was just as valid as mine. In psychiatric parlance, Mason was "atypical," but sometimes atypical is fresh and exciting, and explodes the expectations of convention. Mason reminded me normal is subjective. I wish I could have perceived my sexuality as accurately and honestly as Mason perceived my door.

I loved the job and those kids but looking back I could see myself falling into the same trap I did with the campers, almost over-identifying with them, seeing my role as more important than it was. You had to care, but also accept the limits of what could be accomplished. Over time, I learned it was better for the kids if I spent less time with them and more time helping their parents. That was going to make the biggest difference in their lives, not the hour of therapy with me. If you want to advocate for a kid, advocate for their family. I got rave reviews. The program director told me I was a star, one of the best fellows he ever had, with a promising career ahead of me.

Then why was I so sad and lonely? Being around all those kids just reminded me how desperately I wanted to have children of my own, and a family. On Friday nights I would go out for pizza and beers with the guys, but after a few hours it was time to go home. And suddenly, it seemed everyone had someone else to go home to except me. And my secret life expanded to fit the vacuum.

Technology advanced. VCRs and Betamax emerged. Overnight it seemed, you could rent any film you liked, and my prowling evolved from bookstores to video stores. While at the main Portland Public Library near Pioneer Square, I chanced upon a VHS copy of *The Orphan*, a Russian film about homeless kids in the wake of WWII. There was some casual juvenile nudity. The nudity was incidental for the plot, but I did not watch these films for plot. It was distributed by a company called Award Films, located in West Hollywood. They gave an address for a catalog, which I requested. It was the beginning of a much more intense interest in sexual objectification of children. I convinced myself it was legal, it was innocent, and that I could control it.

I know part of the reason I went into psychiatry was hoping I could find a solution to my troubling sexuality. I think a lot of men join the priesthood for similar reasons, hoping God will have the answer. But it turns out that neither the church nor psychiatry has anything to say about people like us other than "Ick," and then silence.

OHSU had a great psychiatry department, caring and progressive, but as doctors we were on the mountain looking down. During orientation on the first day of residency, one of the senior lecturers popped his head into the room, wild, looking like Albert Einstein on a bad hair day. He gave us one impassioned phrase of advice: "Don't fuck your patients," and fled. Slowly over time I deduced that a previous resident had seduced a woman he was seeing in therapy. He was still on the faculty, but it had caused a scandal. We talked about the sexual issues of patients, how they might be attracted to us, but we never mentioned it could go the other way around. That was too uncomfortable. We talked a lot about depression, but when a third-year resident killed himself by taking pills after locking himself in the trunk of his car, we had a brief memorial, but there was no introspection. It was just something that happens. Institutions are just like people; we look away individually and collectively. I knew I was troubled. I was sad, drinking episodically, and even saw a therapist and got started on Prozac myself, which helped. But I could not be honest about the real pain in my heart. I was too scared. I could lose everything. My dad had warned me about what would happen if anyone caught me doing "that" again. I had it under control, I loved kids and never wanted to hurt them, ever. How bad could it get?

A week later the catalog from Award Films came, and life became simultaneously both better and worse.

Book Adventures, the company which published the photo book *The Boy* I mentioned earlier, advertised their offering as innocent paean to the natural beauty of boys. Pedophilia has existed for millennia. There will always be people like me, and there will always be people who market to people like me. The nudity in the book was not casual or accidental, it was the whole point of the book. A copy of *The Boy* was found at Michael Jackson's Neverland Ranch. That was not random. The ultimate market for *The Boy* is pedophiles.

The same was true for Award Films. They created a catalog specifically for "boylovers," even if they never explicitly used the term. They did the collecting for you by putting together a catalog where the only common denominator was that they depicted attractive boys or very young men. They would "warn" you in their descriptions that the movies offered were "controversial" and might contain "mild to moderate nudity" as though that was a potential downside instead of its *raison d'etre*. The goal of Award Films was to distribute films that come as close as possible to exploitation without crossing the threshold of legality. My reptilian brain thought the gates of heaven had opened wide.

Award offered nudist films (theirs always featured kids), but also spotlighted films dealing with teenage sexuality. The highlight one month was *You Are Not Alone*. It is a Danish film about a sexual and romantic relationship between a twelve and a fourteen-year-old, both of whom are gorgeous. Just the picture of the two boys embracing made me dizzy. I knew ordering from them was also a crossing of some sort, into a presumptively legal but morally questionable domain, but my desire was overwhelming. What I was unable to do on my own was visualize where I was headed. All I knew was that I loved the pictures in the catalog, wanted more, and never wanted anyone else to know.

I anxiously awaited the film's arrival, compulsively checking the mailbox daily. My hands trembled when I finally retrieved it from my mailbox. I breathlessly loaded it into my VCR, then pressed play. I was entranced. There was some nudity, but not much. However it felt like a genuine love story. In the final scene, they boys passionately kiss. It was and is the most erotic thing I have ever seen.

I do not want to have sex with minors. I want to be one of the minors having sex. And I love to watch. But the intensity of the desire was and still is at times terrifying. The irrational power of looking hijacks everything else; time, food, responsibilities, and morals all fade away when I am in the thrall of lust. As usual, after masturbating to an image of a minor, I throw the film away, and I have thrown *You Are Not Alone* away several times, but I always know where to find it again, and my shame over loving it is limited. (Interestingly, one of Jackson's songs is titled "You Are Not Alone," perhaps a coincidence, but I doubt it). What is hateful about lust is that it is never satisfied, one door leads to another, and the door almost always leads to a staircase descending into darkness. I admit that I still love that movie, but my life might have been better if I had never seen it.

A few months before finishing residency, I found myself attending a conference in San Francisco. I had never seen the city before and went exploring. The 360-degree vista from Russian Hill was magnificent. It was spring and flowering trees and shrubs were everywhere. The early evening was warm, but a lovely ocean breeze kept it from becoming uncomfortable. The Golden Gate Bridge in one direction. The Bay Bridge in the other. It was Edenic.

But as I looked over that gorgeous bay on a perfect day in a beautiful city, healthy, young, and secure in a good career, all I could think of was how sad it was that I had no one to share my life with. I talked it over with my dear friends back in Portland.

Brian asked the right question; "Jim, what are you really looking for in a relationship?" The more I thought about it, the more I realized I just wanted someone kind and funny and gentle. Someone like my friend Fran back in medical school. After graduation Fran had gone off to Jefferson Medical College in Philadelphia, where she did her training in internal medicine, the basic care of adults. We were always great friends and kept in touch, and I somehow knew she was as confused in her own way as I was. Whenever we talked, we would confide in how lonely we both were. The dating scene was as uncomfortable and humiliating to her as it was for me. She told me that most unmarried men were coarse and vain and that she was resigned to a solitary life, whose sole non-medical function was to live with and care for her now elderly parents; the role they had always envisioned for her.

I knew there was no passion between us, but by now we were both in our early thirties. It felt like life had an expiration date for happiness that was fast approaching. Why be miserable apart when we could perhaps cobble a better future together? Sexual demands would be limited for us both, and I though a relationship grounded in kindness and friendship could prove durable. Yes it was cold and calculating, but it made a certain desperate sense as a solution for our mutually forlorn state.

Fran and I had talked on the phone many times since we left Syracuse, but after encouragement from the love gurus, I inserted a new urgency into our conversations. I confirmed she was not dating anyone and had no clear prospects on the radar. I wondered whether she was gay, but she demurred. We agreed that I would fly out to Philadelphia for a week, and we would try to be together to explore whether there was a foundation we could build from.

This was not how it was supposed to work. My naïve understanding was that people's eyes meet across the room like Zeffirelli's *Romeo and Juliet,* or you were Michael Corleone in *The Godfather* and got hit by "The Thunderbolt." But literature also provided the beloved marriage plots of Jane Austen, which portrayed matchmaking as a combination of chess match and business negotiation. I failed at Shakespearian ardor; let's see how friendship fared.

She was as excited to see me as I was to see her. I paid my air fare.

She paid for a room at the Bentley Hotel on Rittenhouse Square. Truth is, I had forgotten how beautiful she is when her face lights up with a smile. We had coffee and scones at the Reading Terminal Market the night I arrived and made plans to visit her apartment and have dinner the next evening.

She was more scared than I was. "I am poison" she told me the next evening although I still have no idea what she meant by that. An interval of two months had elapsed between our initial discussion and my actual arrival into town, and both of us had erected towers of fear and fantasy. The first night I was there, I put on my best suit, and we went out to Girasole, a wonderful romantic restaurant. There I told her I still thought we were great friends and I wanted to return to the good days in Syracuse. "But Jimmy, I am supposed to take care of Mama and Papa, and Peter and Shole (her siblings) are the ones who are supposed to get married. My parents think you are a grifter and will just leave me. Are you certain we should be doing this?" I was gripped by an overwhelming sense that it was now or never for me; either I plunge headfirst into the murky water below or spend the rest of my life stuck on the top of the cliff wondering what diving feels like. I had this inexplicable sense this was my sole chance at happiness, and I told her so. "I think we should be together, forever." I think she had the same sense of being on a precipice, and we agreed to live together. I had never even kissed her and spent that night staring at the ceiling back at the Bentley thinking, hoping, praying I had done something good.

The next morning, we set off for the Philadelphia Zoo, both of us euphoric over the idea that perhaps we were not destined to grow old alone. In an hour we were deliriously naming our future offspring. We were both going so fast, and so blind. I almost instantaneously panicked. What was I getting myself into? That was the weirdest, wildest, most exhilarating, and simultaneously terrifying five days of my life. We were engaged, broken up, and engaged again in between Monday and Friday. There were things said and things left unsaid, but odd as it is we may have as good a relationship as any couple I know, and we have been through a lot.

Both of us were terrified by sex. My guess is that Fran has some old trauma she does not remember or has chosen not to deal with, so it was even worse for her than for me. We tried to fumble through it. It was something we needed to do more than wanted to do. I really do not much enjoy "normal" sex. For Fran I can only guess. She just tells me she does not feel "normal" and leaves it at that. But I did love sharing a world with another human being. Her kind brother Peter wanted his beloved Frannie to be happy and treated us to a Philadelphia Eagles game. We had Pat's cheesesteaks and listened to jazz at Zanzibar Blues. I loved having my friend back. I loved going for walks. I loved putting my head in her lap.

My single greatest regret in my life is my inability to be honest with my best friend. She deserved full disclosure. She deserved to know I had little to no sexual attraction to adults. She deserved to know "I was poison."

Would she have married me if she knew? I am not sure I want to know the answer to that question.

Chapter 9

Billings

I returned from Philadelphia eager to tell Terry and Brian of my half-planned, half-impulsive engagement. They were less troubled than I was by the unconventional nature of my romance. They knew convention was overrated.

In June 1994, Fran and I got married near Portland at the site of the old Multnomah County tuberculosis hospital, now converted to a winery. Except for her brother Peter, no one from Fran's family attended. After we were married, there were some basic skills we both had to work on. Fran never learned how to drive; it was not a skill Persian women were expected to master, and it was a terrifying experience to learn it while negotiating Portland traffic. For my part, I had to learn to share space, physical and emotional, instead of allowing myself to get lost in daydreams.

Fran's parents never expected her to become independent and leave the nest once residency was done. She surrendered family ties by marrying me. It was a huge sacrifice, and as we thought about our life together, it made sense that we should not remain in Portland, which was my town, or return to Philadelphia, which was her town. Instead, we would find a place to be our town. We both needed physical and emotional distance from our respective families, so staying out west made sense. Idealistically I wanted to go somewhere that really needed me. Oregon had a good number of child psychiatrists; I wanted to go someplace relatively underserved.

Fran and I took a year to explore the country, working as locum tenens doctors, traveling from state to state to take temporary jobs for a month or two. On one of my trips I passed through Billings, Montana. From a very young age, I had been enthralled by mountains and wilderness, and Montana has both in superabundance. Billings was the right-sized town, not too big nor too small. It had a new psychiatric hospital, so there were some resources, but there were only a handful of psychiatrists in the entire state. There would be more than enough to do. I was also assured there would be a place for Fran.

In July 1994, I started working at the local clinic. I spent the first month or two muddling through paperwork and a non-intuitive dictation system. I won the lottery when Maggie Barovich was assigned as my nurse, a realization that became more and more apparent over time. She was a smart, tough North Dakota ranch girl who went to nursing school when the graduates still took an oath to be faithful to the profession and obedient to their physician. Maggie was the heart and soul of our practice. I have never known anyone to better combine clinical wisdom with good common sense. She made the appointments, called in the scripts, and calmed the daily storms that rained down on our little practice. Often when I asked her how her afternoon went she replied, "I spent it all listening to crying mothers."

With ten years of experience, she knew the medications, dosing, and common side effects of our usual medications better than I did. In the first few weeks, I insisted on hand-writing every prescription. This required copying out the medication name, strength, directions, and number of refills, followed by a signature. Maggie told me that was a waste of time and that I just needed to sign a blank pad of scripts and let her fill in the rest. I was horrified at the thought of anyone writing prescriptions under my name. But after a week I realized I made more careless mistakes (such as a wrong date or misspelled name) than she did. I learned to do as I was told. Those were more innocent days, before we worried someone would steal our blank prescriptions, and pre-signing pads was common; later this practice would be banned. Thereafter, I would let her fill out the body of the scripts and sign them *en masse* at the end of the day.

CHAPTER 9 – BILLINGS

We were the lone psychiatric hospital for eastern Montana and northern Wyoming; a catchment area the size of New England. The only other child psychiatrist the clinic employed was Luke Zinsser, a larger-than-life teddy bear of a man who loved to hunt, fish, and live exuberantly. He grew up near Louisville, not far from the area in Kentucky my family was from, but he stayed country gentry, whereas I was always going to be a city slicker. He was a wonderful hard-working doctor, albeit with a touch of attention deficit-hyperactivity disorder (ADHD) himself, great with families and utterly sincere about helping children. Those intense over-whelming years working with Luke and Maggie were the best of my career, and I treasure them, and my good fortunate to have known them as colleagues.

No one brings their child to a psychiatrist joyfully. It usual-ly occurs after defeat. A suicide attempt. An assault in school. Uncontrollable behavior at home. You do not make an appointment with a child psychiatrist because you want to, but because you must.

Before becoming my nurse Maggie, had worked for a retired pe-diatrician in town who specialized in ADHD, and soon all those patients migrated to me, mostly because they were attached to Maggie. But we were soon besieged with hordes of new referrals, many of which were "rule out ADHD" evaluations. Parents would come to the office in despair. Their child was failing and getting into trouble in class and on the playground. Homework and chores were a nightmare. In my initial ninety-minute appointment I would try to figure out what was going on, make a diagnosis, and start treatment if appropriate.

There are many reasons why children struggle with attention. Sometimes the work is too easy, and they are bored. Sometimes the work is too hard, and they are overwhelmed. Occasionally there were underlying medical issues. We made several diagnoses of ab-sence ("petit mal") seizures when we noticed fluttering eyelids or a blank stare after asking the child to hyperventilate, a sign that suggests brief but frequent epileptic activity. The toughest diag-nostic dilemma was differentiating kids with intrinsic attention issues (ADHD) from kids that who could not focus because they were anxious and traumatized. ADHD kids are born more active, impulsive, and distractible than the average child. But they get distracted by things outside of their brain; a bird on the playground, someone sharpening their pencil, the boy in the seat next to them passing gas. Anxious, traumatized kids get distracted from things inside their brain, such as memories of the past, or realistic fears for the future. You have to make an accurate diagnosis or your treatment will not be effective, and worse, you will be neglecting the underlying problem.

It is rare in childhood mental health for medication to be the treatment of choice, but that is the case with ADHD, and why kids ended up in our clinic rather than in therapy. Giving psychiatric medication to children is serious business. A common misconception is that parents just want to "drug" their kids with Ritalin or Adderall so teachers do not have to teach and parents do not have to parent. Nothing is further from the truth. Parents hate giving unnecessary medications to their kids and kids hate taking them.

My job was not to tell anyone what to do; my job was to empower parents with accurate information and give them reasonable options. If the diagnosis was ADHD I would explain the genetic nature of the condition, that it was not due to bad parenting or willful naughtiness, that it runs a predictable course, and that there were risks to treatment and risks to non-treatment.

I tried to impart to parents that although medicine was the cornerstone of effective treatment, behavioral strategies regarding discipline and organization were also essential for a positive outcome. We tried very hard to solicit feedback from teachers and the schools. By the time I left the clinic I think I had attended meetings at every school in Yellowstone County.

When medicine was prescribed, we tried to use the lowest effective dose, and emphasized we were using medicine as a helpful tool, not for "mind control." I would tell my patients "I do not have any medication that will force you to do what I want you to, if I did, my lawn would be mowed more regularly than it is. The goal is to enable you to do what you want to do, so you can make the adults in your life happier and have more fun." I also told people that this medicine worked fast, we would know very quickly if it helped, and if it did not, I was probably on the wrong track.

There is nothing more gratifying than effective treatment of ADHD in children who thought they were failures. The kid who never got recess because he never finished his work gets to play. The kid who got F's because she never handed in homework or rushed through her tests ends up with A's and B's. The kid who never listens when chores come up, does what is asked, and gets praised instead of scolded. Elementary school kids want very badly to be good. If they are not being good, it is simply because they do not know how. There is no better feeling in the world than having a kid running to your office excitedly with a terrific school report in their hand while listening to a parent tell you, "Doc, I had my doubts about trying it, but I have to admit it, Christopher listens better, is happier, and likes school again."

I am not saying that happened every time, or that the medicines are perfect. And no medicine lasts forever, but when you have been successful once, you know you can be successful again. We always knew those kids were smart and capable. But they themselves often despaired of ever being successful. That changed.

I adored those kids, and usually got to see them at their best, since even I can usually keep children from being bored for a half-hour. They were lively, curious, and never forgot that I had hot chocolate with mini marshmallows hidden somewhere in the staff room. They were some of the best kids in the world. I loved being part of their success.

We were a general child psychiatric clinic and saw kids who were bipolar, depressed, aggressive, and anxious. They did not respond to medical interventions in such a quick, gratifying way as the uncomplicated ADHD cases. Rewards and challenges came with every new referral.

Up to a third of our patients were foster kids. Maggie and I felt these children were our highest priority. They always were first off the waiting list. Most of the kids were in the system because their parents had substance abuse problems or their own serious mental illness. The parents were often neglected and abused by their own parents growing up, which left them vulnerable to inflicting the same damage on their children. Effective intervention in the cycle of multi-generational trauma is the critical mental health challenge of our time. Multi-generational trauma wraps its tendrils around all aspects of society and when left untreated, worsens physical health, educational/occupation outcomes, and directly leads to high levels of antisocial behavior often driven by substance use. It is a persistent, remorseless foe and we saw its dark reverberations daily.

We had kids who would not go to school. We had kids who wanted to blow the school up. We had kids who never slept without a knife under their pillow.

The hardest ones were the ones who had been abandoned or neglected when they were infants or toddlers—the unattached kids. Sometimes they had been beaten or savagely abused. One of the most disturbing referrals I ever got came from urology, after they had removed several two-inch needles that had been inserted into the urethra of a first grader.

Many of these children were physically and emotionally abandoned, which is every bit as damaging as physical or sexual trauma. It was common for toddlers to be given a bottle and left to fend for themselves, their caretakers too strung out or passed out. In the late 1990s and early 2000s overwhelming waves of illegal drug use surged through eastern Montana, leaving unprecedented numbers of traumatized kids in their wakes, deluging the social service and foster care systems. Preschoolers would be found wandering alone and barefoot downtown. Often the guardians did not even know they were missing.

Entire groups of siblings would get referred to our office, like the Symington kids. Their mother Cindy had been diagnosed with schizophrenia and as a teen runaway herself was well versed in life on the streets. She had three children by James who was never fully in or fully out of her life. Only Cindy's stepmom helped with the kids, so when she died of lung cancer they were on their own. One day Cindy just left the kids with a half-sister while she went out to buy some cigarettes.

She never returned.

At the time Timothy was seven, Leo four, and Laney just one and a half. By then their collective behaviors were so overwhelming the half-sister called child welfare and said she just could not handle them. James had beaten Cindy and was suspected of having something to do with her disappearance, but it could not be proven. What was certain is that he shot a man in a drug deal gone bad down in Greeley and was sentenced to twenty-five years in Limon. Only God and the children themselves knew what they had witnessed and experienced.

That left family services with the unenviable task of finding a foster home for three troubled kids. Providence intervened in the form of Mark and Lisa Lenzi, a childless couple living in a small home in rural Grass Range.

Physically the children presented as healthy, superficially well-behaved, and intelligent. But appearances were deceiving. Timothy was timid and passive, an almost ghost-like presence. He would disappear for hours at a time but could not recall where he had been. He never cried. Leo was cherubic with a bright smile and the longest eyelashes I have ever seen. Again, superficially he was quiet, but long after being toilet trained the family would find urine or even piles of feces in the corner of his bedroom. He also was a talented, dedicated thief, and would hoard items in little secret stashes. Sometimes it was food, which made sense, and sometimes it was random objects, like paperclips or string. A more endearing trait was Leo's devotion to Laney; he always knew where she was. The baby seemed to be the least disturbed of the three, and a blessing and balm to the whole family.

I saw those kids every month or so for a dozen years. There were not a lot of mental health resources in central Montana, and we used everything at our disposal. The Lenzis were such nice people, preternaturally patient and kind, even when problems seemed insurmountable. I so wanted to help them. Individual therapy for the kids seemed an uncertain enterprise at best. Sweet, quiet Timothy got worse when pressed about his feelings, which made sense given how grim some of his memories were. He wrote dark poetry filled with shame and self-hatred he possessed. There were several brief hospitalizations for suicidal behaviors. Medicines were not the answer, but sometimes they took the edge off and made life manageable.

Karate (and the Lenzis' patient kindness) were his salvation. The martial arts allowed him a chance to finally feel comfortable inhabiting his body and endowed him with the confidence that he could defend himself and his family. In a big city, he might have gotten lost in the shuffle, but there is no hiding in a small town in Montana. Slowly, almost imperceptibly he grew in quiet confidence. He was able to form a genuine bond with the Lenzis, who adopted all three kids after a few years. It took many months, but he slowly learned to tolerate physical contact, and even a bit of affection. Remembering him slowly sidle up to his father puts a smile on my face to this day. He is in university up in Missoula.

Leo struggled more. One moment he would be sweet, the next moment he was a Tasmanian devil. After burning down the family barn for no apparent reason he spent a month at the hospital, and then we made the hard decision as a parent-led treatment team to place him in a group home in Helena. Some months went well, others not so much. When upset or triggered he could throw hellacious tantrums which required restraints, sometimes weekly, sometimes daily. I never saw these tantrums in my office, and although we knew each other well, seeing someone so traumatized in person for twenty minutes every month was not enough time for me to really understand his internal world. But he slowly improved, maybe just with maturity, and after several cautious trial visits, was able to return home full time after a few years.

He was in high school and doing better the last time I saw him, but had been caught drinking in class several time. He and I had several heart-to-heart talks about the dangers of alcoholism for hurting kids, and what a trap it could be for him. I have my fingers crossed.

Laney was happy and relatively easy- for whatever reasons (maybe Leo's protection) she seemed to have evaded the long reach of trauma. She was the princess of the family, and she knew it. Although not officially my patient she always accompanied her brothers for their visits to Billings. So, it was a shock when I got an anxious call from Lisa one winter night. Is Timothy suicidal? Did Leo set another fire? No, but Laney was complaining that the books in the library were talking to her and seemed unusually anxious and scared. Over the course of a year, it became depressingly clear that Laney was developing the severe psychotic illness her mother was purported to have. Meds helped, but she gained a lot of weight, and required more parenting over time, not less.

Working with families like the Lenzis through good times and bad. Developing relationships. Being there, even when I had no easy answers. That was my job. I want to tell you I loved it, and I did.

What I do not want to tell you is how emotionally draining it was, how ineffective I frequently felt, and how desperate I was to feel something different, anything different once I hung up the phone and the long day was done.

Chapter 10

Family

Although we were not the world's most conventional couple, Fran and I easily transitioned into family life. Neither of us had any savings so we rented a cheap little one-bedroom apartment on Lancelot Lane at the Castle Rock Apartments outside of town. At least it had a little outdoor pool so Fran could soak while waiting for the state medical board to finish processing her license. The apartment walls were the thickness of prison toilet paper, so you heard everyone and everything. While I worked, Frannie quickly assumed her natural role as world's best neighbor and after a few days everyone was dropping by with medical questions, relationship concerns, and pleas for emergency babysitting.

The two of us were new to the whole domesticity scene. We scoured the thrift stores for used furniture, and I spent most of those first weekends assembling cheap plywood TV stands and cabinets. Given my limited practical skills, it should be no surprise that the finished products looked nothing like the pictures on the box. I never seemed to have the right number of screws or dowels, and in my frustration found myself cursing like a sailor, much to the delight of the urchins eavesdropping in the apartments adjacent, who giggled and echoed my oaths.

Fran had never cooked, but gamely took it up. After one long day at the hospital, I returned home to a medley of baked, breaded fish, packaged mac and cheese, and frozen carrots. Remarkably each dish exactly resembled the others in color and texture. Fran called it her monochrome meal. I referred to it as her *hommage a l'orange*.

After supper, we would meander our way through our new neighborhood and depending on the weather, we might see a neon red-yellow sunset over the Beartooth Mountains or watch a distant thunderstorm roll up the prairie towards our coulee.

After a couple months Fran got her license, happily went back to work ("Jimmy, I never claimed to be a *hausfrau*") and life settled into a pleasant, busy rhythm. We fumbled in the bedroom. I love Fran, and I know she loves me, but physical intimacy was awkward for both of us. Fran would just tell me she was not a very sexual person, which I at least partially believe. I certainly had my own problems, and was in no position to complain, so avoiding intimacy came easily and naturally.

I remember those first two years in the Heights fondly. We bought our first new cars, learned how to dig out of Montana snowstorms (Syracuse had more accumulation, but it also had more snowplows), and decorated our first miniature Christmas tree, even though we were both pagans at best.

After a year or two we saved enough money to make a down payment on a home closer to the hospital we did not have to share a wall with twenty neighbors. The children of the complex were distressed that we were moving, Fran knew all their birthdays, and was a conspicuous soft touch.

We bought a lovely, sensible middle-class house on the west side of town. at thirty-five (medical training lasts a long time), we were finally grown up and independent.

Next step: baby. It was very clear to both of us that a major goal of marriage was to start a family. I wanted a child very badly; Fran wanted one even more. Again, like the anatomy test, how difficult could it be? We were both awkward and anxious, instead of spontaneously joyful. We tried to have fun, but the clear goal of the activity was procreation. I am not sure I really needed the Viagra I would sneak surreptitiously from the drug sample closet, but it boosted my confidence.

Getting older reduces everyone's fertility rate. It can be the bane of younger physicians. There you are in your mid-to-late thirties, finally not required to work in the hospital every third night, eager to catch up on lost time, only to have your body betray you. Having had no initial success at conception and conscious that the ticking hands of our reproductive clocks were rapidly winding down, we consulted with a fertility specialist, who initiated a routine work up.

The man's job is relatively simple. In the fertility clinic's mens room were several well-worn magazines on a cabinet next to the specimen bottle. The first *Playboys* I had seen in years. Like old home week.

Of course, because life is nothing if not consistently unfair, the woman's lot is much more fraught with a host of blood draws, x-rays, and unpleasant poking and prodding.

At first we were told not to worry too much, we had only been at this for a year or two and being anxious lowers the success rate. Upon being told anxiety made it worse, we became very anxious about our collective anxiety.

We needed to have sex around Fran's ovulation, as measured by daily basal temperatures. Fran would come on the appointed day, announce "Doctor's Orders" and we would decamp to the bedroom.

Forty-eight hours later Fran would go into the bathroom, testing kit in hand, only to sadly emerge twenty minutes later. It is such a cruel emotional experience. Sometimes she would cry quietly, and I would try to assure her we would get through it together, and not to despair.

Providentially, just before we were set to fly to Denver for a procedure, the strip turned blue. I have never seen Frannie happier than when holding that pregnancy test in her hand. It was around our second Thanksgiving together, and it was hard to keep the secret. Three weeks later we finally bought *What to Expect When You Are Expecting* and started making plans for the best Christmas ever. A week later was the Internal Medicine Holiday Party. We were all happy and dolled up for the party, so I was shocked when Fran came up to me in the middle of it looking agitated and pale "Jimmy, we must go home right now. I'm bleeding, heavily." We lost the baby that night.

The spring was hard. Fran had made the mistake of telling

everyone she knew the second her test was positive. Now she had to take it back. What really helped was our kind obstetrician re-assuring us that if Fran got pregnant once, it just proved it could be done and we needed to persist. But it was always on our minds.

My storytelling brain thinks this was the time I started more than casual drinking, but that may be too glib and convenient to be entirely true.

There had been a minimum food charge at the inn where we had our wedding, but since our reception was a small one, by the time it was over we still possessed a thousand-dollar credit which they honored with cases of wine. I had never really been a big drinker up until then, but I soon found wine was a wonderful way to disappear.

I started with just a glass or two on the weekends. I knew Dad was an alcoholic who drank vodka to get drunk. I would sample wine as an epicurean, a sophisticated part of a sophisticated lifestyle. It became my new obsession. I subscribed to magazines, started going to wine tastings, and began my own pilgrimages to liquor stores, buying expensive vintages by the case. Even though we were not wealthy, in about two years, I went from hardly drinking at all to having three hundred bottles stored in the basement, and I went from a glass or two to a bottle or two every evening.

Not real bright.

I seem to love collecting, whether it is stamps, wine, or films. I loved the wine porn ("A full bodied voluptuous red with tantalizing notes of ripe blackberries, sensuously redolent of leath-er and luscious figs"). I would memorize varietals, vintages, and terroir. I was not a drunk. I was a connoisseur who just happened to always get drunk. The first glass or two were all about the nose, the mouthfeel, and the complexity of taste. But I never stopped at a glass or two. After forty minutes I just wanted to be plastered, to not feel anxious, to not feel. Uncomfortable sexual thoughts and wine went together like kites and wind. Wine made me feel less guilty about my daily thoughts, where I was not always playing the role of a good straight husband. It soothed and reassured me and made it easier to fall asleep, even if the sleep was poor. It let me forget my self-contradictions, at least for a while.

Fran and I were again discussing in vitro. It was an expensive procedure, but the money was not the problem, it was the incessant courting of failure. It all felt so personal for her. "Jimmy, I understand if you want to leave me for someone who can give you children."

Of course, I wanted children, but not as much as I wanted Fran to be happy, and to know, truly know, that I cherished her love and friendship, and that I instinctively knew what it felt like to feel broken from birth.

A few weeks later Fran again became pregnant. This time we told no one for weeks. In June 1997, Fran gave birth to our only child Bridget. The best things come to those who wait.

To say that a first baby changes your life is an age-old cliché. But oh Lord, does a first baby ever change your life. How could something so tiny and seemingly helpless completely transform my house and my world in less than a week? It was like a tornado, but one you welcomed instead of feared. At first, we were inundated with baby clothing as everybody in town finally got to reciprocate Fran's generosity. I do not believe Bridget wore the same outfit twice for the first year of her life.

I loved being a father. Fran was morning minion. I was evening minion.

Of course, I always had a rocking chair and I would get to administer the before bed bottle. Bridget has her mother's beautiful big brown eyes, and my straight hair. Gazing into her eyes while feeding her was the purest moments of joy in my life. She was always so easy. My partner Luke called her the "perfect child," and of course he was right.

When Fran worked on the weekends it was just Bridge and me. We would go on little expeditions. I remember taking her to the zoo one windy Saturday. I had exited the car and prepared to retrieve Bridget from her car seat in back when a sudden gust blew the driver's side door shut. In the tumult of collecting the stroller and necessary accoutrements I had left the keys in the car, locking Bridget inside. I frantically ran from the parking lot to the zoo office and told them to call the fire department, that I had inadvertently locked my daughter in our car, and then rushed back to Bridget. I thought she would be crying, as upset and hysterical as I was, but she just thought it was a fun game and gazed at me beatifically through the window. She loved seeing the fire truck. She thought it was our best trip ever.

She adored visiting and being with people. I remember taking her trick or treating one cold Halloween; she might have been five at the time. We had been out for over an hour, and it was snowing (we are talking Montana here). I asked her if she wanted to go home to a warm fire, but she gently but firmly demurred, "Daddy, I am having fun. Let's go visit more friendly neighbors."

As a little girl she was more her mother's daughter. We were hiking in spectacular Glacier National Park one bright autumn afternoon and the car was parked a little further away than she was comfortable with which led to the comment of "Dad, why are we always hiking? You know I am a girly girl. I just want to go to the mall." On another afternoon, I pretended we were lost in the woods, and she remonstrated me with "You got us lost, now you are going to have to capture animals, make a fire, and built me a house."

But as she got older, I could see my genetic influence. She played soccer through third grade, but aggression did not come naturally. When a ball appeared between her and an opponent, she always deferred to her friend with the different colored jersey. Competition had no allure; her greatest pleasure during the game was just to visit with friends on the sidelines.

Miraculously I had cobbled together the life and the family I dreamed of. Maybe it was too good to be true, or maybe deep down I did not feel I deserved this life. All I know is that I could not shake my stubborn streak of obsessive self-destruction.

My sexual thoughts of boys never went away. I could tamp them down with work, family, or wine, but sooner or later I would get restless and entitled, hoping I could touch the hot stove without getting burned. Occasionally I would order a movie or two from Award. The advertisements appeared in generic plain manila envelopes and were easy to conceal. I would hide the films and objectify to them when Fran was on call, particularly before the baby was born. I always felt guilty, but thought I was keeping my secret life under control. In fact, my contradictions were killing me. I looked good from the outside, but I was dogged by chronic headaches and a gnawing stomach pain that never went away. My life was like a child's balloon—sooner or later it would slip my grasp and fly away.

For ten years I served as the psychiatric consultant for Pine Hills Youth Correctional Facility. Initially known as the State Boys School, Pine Hills was where the powers that be sent delinquent and un-governable young men and served as a combination reform school/orphanage for many years. By the time they hired me, it was in the process of becoming a formal part of the Department of Corrections with locks, walls, and barbed wire. Every three weeks or so, I would drive down to Miles City, a cowboy town if ever there was one, and spend a day or two seeing any kid the nursing or counseling staff thought might benefit from psychiatric consultation or medication.

Those were some of the saddest, most mistreated kids on earth. The infirmary was the one place they could come for a little care and concern, particularly from our first-rate nursing staff. Theoretically mentally ill kids were not supposed to be at Pine, but it happened all the time. Where else are you going to put an aggressive boy with a severe mood disorder that no long-term psychiatric hospital wants to deal with? Our goal was to limit the number of medications, while also limiting the number of physical injuries to kids and staff. It was the one time I would chemically restrain kids with powerful meds, just to prevent them from cutting themselves or assaulting others. We did the best we could with counseling and therapy but some of those boys were so damaged. I remember one cold-eyed young man guaranteeing me he would kill before he tuned twen-ty-one. Sometimes line staff thought we were being too nice to the kids ("hugs for thugs"), but in general, our efforts were appreci-ated, and I felt valued and useful.

I was surprised when a few years into my contract the state decid-ed to develop a treatment program on the campus for teens who had committed sexual offenses. They were getting more and more of these kids and sending them out of state was financially prohibitive. It was the first time I realized there might be some sort of treatment for sexual offenses. Those boys possessed overwhelming shame and self-loathing. We housed murderers (rarely) and assaultive kids (often). One boy stole an airplane; everyone called him "Aviator." But none of them had the sadness and despair of the boys on the sex offender unit. Many of them were there for molesting younger siblings or cousins; most had been sexually abused themselves, usually at an early age. It was so hard to talk about, but it became clear that the only way you ever got better was to talk about it.

Back in my office in Billings, I would occasionally get an intake for a child who was sexually acting out. I am not sure I was very helpful. One twelve-year-old kept getting caught fondling peers on the bus and on the playground. He lived in a farm community in the far northwest part of the state, three hundred miles from my office. We had telemedicine visits once a month. I think I am a decent therapist and a kind man, but I did not have the skills to engage a sexually reactive kid via teleconferencing. All I could do was remind him he could not act the way he was acting, or he was going to end up in an institution. Of course, shaming him just made it worse, but I truly did not know what else to do. It felt as though we almost had to wait to have him adjudicated to Pine Hills before we could give him the intense treatment he needed. As a society we do not communicate to teenagers that it is okay to have uncomfortable sexual thoughts and feelings, and that you can get help for them.

Joshua was fifteen and referred by his family because the FBI had come to their house intending to arrest his father for downloading child pornography, which at the time I did not even know was obtainable. But when the police got there, it turned out that the son was downloading it, not the father, and it all involved children younger than my patient. Looking back, Joshua was likely a budding pedophile, and my heart went out to him. But I got nowhere with that kid; he could not talk about how he felt to save his soul. Whenever I brought up the pornography he just blushed, lowered his face, and clammed up.

We can deplore sexual crimes, but we cannot be surprised by their dogged persistence in the world. And we cannot pray or wish them away.

Pine Hills had a more effective plan. Visit the kids every day, have groups every week. Do not focus on the crime, focus on their life, and the reasons for acting out will become apparent. Talk about normal sexuality as if you are teaching a class, so as not to make everyone defensive, separate the offender from their offense, and over time progress does occur. But it requires such hard work from the staff, and such hard work from the boys. They had to talk about their own vulnerabilities, their fears, their rage, and their despair of being able to control their bodies. I focused on medication management and although I did not directly participate in treatment, I visited the kids every month and saw how they grew and matured emotionally over years (and it took years).

Those kids tried to cover sadness with bravado; we had boys who would cut deep ugly gashes in their arms and legs or knock their heads against concrete walls so violently they gave themselves concussions. Self-inflicted physical pain was preferable to the emotional pain they carried every day. Only by facing searing emotional pain could true growth proceed. Not everyone was capable of such honesty and acceptance

I was copying those self-mutilators; except I used wine and porn instead of razors. I did not yet possess the bravery and gift of desperation of the boys at Pine Hills, but they showed me what it might look like.

At night I still pray that I helped my patients half as much as they helped me.

Chapter 11

Drowning

The internet began to intrude into my consciousness in the late 90s. I ditched the Apple IIc I bought to play video games when I was in medical school and switched to an expensive Gateway model so I could upgrade my gaming experience. However, you could not avoid the omnipresent advertisements for America Online (AOL), and the internet seemed exciting and inevitable. So I went down to Western Technology Partners in downtown Billings, plunked down my hundred bucks, picked up the six floppy discs required to install the program, and logged into a brave new world.

At first it was confusing, and seemingly pointless. Connecting required a modem and the data transfer speed maxed out at 26k/second, lightning at the time but still painfully slow. Every webpage took several minutes to download and display, and it all seemed like junk. Most of the early sites were simply advertisements for the company that owned them. Why bother with commercials on the internet when you could see them on TV? But slowly the power of obtaining information in real time dawned on me. I could get the scores of the Browns and the Indians instantaneously, no longer having to wait for SportsCenter. If I wanted information on a band or (of course) a wine, it was at my fingertips.

The process was a bit cumbersome. You would try to connect to your modem. At first all you heard was dialing in the background. Sometimes the lines were busy, and it hung up; other times mechanical chirps, buzzes, and clicks let you know you were connected, leading to a loading screen. Initially I used the computer mostly to play fantasy games like *Daggerfall,* but over time I started using AOL to surf news and sports sites. The AOL home screen displayed several tabs, one entitled "Newsgroups" and one day I impulsively clicked it.

Newsgroups were a big part of the nascent world wide web, essentially a collection of text messages for any conceivable interest. Over time the technology developed so that text messages could link to songs, photographs, or even videos, tasks now facilitated by Pinterest or YouTube. The big difference was that newsgroups were not censored or moderated. If you liked muscle cars, you could search for '66 Mustangs and find a newsgroup devoted to that car and everyone who loved them. I am a huge Brian Wilson/Beach Boys nerd. We all have songs that speak to us. *In My Room* and *I Just Wasn't Made for These Times* are two of my favorites, so I typed in "Beach Boys" looking for some live versions. The search resulted in "alt. fan.beachboys" but there were unexpected results as well, including groups with names like "alt.binaries.pictures.boys" and "alt.fan. prettyboy." One click connected to thousands of "posts." A post was just one line of text; sometimes it made sense, sometimes it was gibberish like "abb42.jpg." It took me a while to figure out "jpg" was a file extension for images. Click on "donsmustang.jpg", and you would get a photo of Don's newest automotive acquisition. But if you clicked on "abb42.jpg" from a group like alt.binaries.pictures. boys you might well get a picture of a gorgeous teen wearing just a speedo, or even less.

The early internet was lawless. Thankfully, it is much more regulated now. I never hear about newsgroups anymore, and if they exist, they require special software and obscure websites to access. There will always be illegal pornography on the internet. I have not seen illegal pornography for more than ten years and do not want to know how to currently find it, but back then you could access those newsgroups in five to ten clicks of the mouse straight from the AOL loading screen.

The early internet was slow. A picture did not appear instantly like it does now. The loading process pantomimed a striptease, revealing the image a bit at a time. Was it a picture of a boy? Was he at the age I most craved, between ten and fourteen. Was he cute? Was he shirtless? If he were wearing a swimsuit, could I see his butt or his bulge?

I could comb bookstores for hours searching for a book or two that might have one black and white picture of an attractive boy. Now there were thousands of free color images more candid than anything I ever dreamed of, at my fingertips, for free, and best of all, downloaded in what I foolishly imagined was total anonymity. Heaven and hell appeared simultaneously. I was thrilled and appalled, exultant and despondent. My worst nightmare came true. I got what I always wanted.

For me, the newsgroups were crack cocaine, and I was hopelessly hooked, almost overnight. It was like being able to be in the shower rooms with boys again, but these were anonymous boys. I had nothing to do with them. They were just pictures. They did not know I was there in front of my computer, a creepy graying man in his mid-forties. Of course, I knew it was bad, I knew it right from the start, but I loved it so. And it was secret, my secret. I rapidly lost the ability to make rational choices.

I was doomed. Even that first night, I had an intimation I was planting the seeds of my inevitable destruction, but I was drowning in a tsunami of desire I could not escape.

The next four years are hazy. I would try to be a normal guy Monday through Friday, and stay away from the computer, but would binge on wine and porn most weekends. I spent less time with my family; they were fine on their own. Friday nights, Fran and Bridget would be asleep early. I would start drinking my wine and then close the door to the computer room. Fran did not know what I looked at, and I would have done anything to keep my secret. I became euphoric just pulling out the cork, taking the first sip of alcohol while anticipating the magic sound of the connected modem, like the instant high a heroin user gets when he sees the backflash of blood in his syringe. I never knew what I would find. Sometimes just pictures of happy boys in swimsuits—and the basic newsgroups rarely had anything else—but I saw that some pictures were cross posted to more than one group, and the other groups had more cryptic names. If you searched them, you would quickly find they were loaded with more graphic content, including pictures from nudist magazines from the 60s and 70s. I had never seen anything like these pictures, and they were obviously sexually exploitative. They were also almost painfully arousing. And there were thousands upon thousands of images. The well had no bottom. Alcohol made it worse; it increased my euphoria while disinhibiting me. My goal was not to orgasm. It was to live in a dissociative fantasy world with just me and my pictures. I wanted to save the images and spend my whole life surrounded by them. I wanted to live forever in somnolent, honeyed pleasure, like the gnat drawn to the nectar of a Venus flytrap.

After an hour or two, my penis sore from rubbing that long, I would climax to a particularly exciting image. I know people struggle with calling compulsive behaviors which involve non-chemical substances (like gambling, food, and sex) addictions. And as someone who has some familiarity with both types, there are differences as well as similarities. You can call it what you want; all I know is that I was hooked. For me, the distinguishing feature of pornography was how quickly and conclusively the spell would end. I was so aroused one second, then after being unable to hold if off one instant longer, I would have cold semen on my hands. The spell and allure of the forbidden vanished instantaneously, and I was left with the reality that I had spent my evening making love to my computer while my wife and daughter slept. Shame and remorse would then sweep down like an avalanche. I would furiously, obsessively delete the files, curse myself for being weak, selfish, and the very picture of a hypocrite. I was fully aware that helping children by day while objectifying them at night was hopelessly contradictory.

Believe me, I tried. I bargained. I would only look at fully clothed boys, and that would last for a few weeks, maybe even a month. I threw my computer away. I cancelled my internet, promising never to go back, yet always going back. Even though I am a psychiatrist, I was not self-knowing enough to intuit the mutually reinforcing connection between alcohol and sex. Maybe I could try and stay away from the computer, but if you also took away wine as well, what was the point of living? This is the madness of addicts, all the commonplace things we love become drab and commonplace when contrasted with addiction. Although I had a good job (which I cared about more than anything, since it was the identity I wanted the world to see), and a better family, which I shamefully neglected during those dark years, the only thing I saw that made life tolerable were the certainty that the weekend was approaching.

Later or sooner, I would get drunk, access something I promised myself I would stay away from, and resume my downward descent. Often the images in the newsgroups would contain links to websites on the regular internet. Sometimes these sites would revolve around boy "models," and for whatever reason most of them seemed to originate from eastern Europe and Russia. My favorite site was Azov Films, based in Toronto. They were the newer and more controversial incarnation of Award Films, and as such would sell clearly legal films like *Stand by Me* along with "legal" but clearly salacious "family nudism films" and photo sets of boy models stored on DVDs. I talked myself into thinking it would be okay if I bought "a film or two," since it would keep me away from the internet and darker images. Any addict knows this never works; switching from vodka to beer because it has less alcohol just makes you drink more beer. And there is never enough beer, just like there is never the perfect image. No matter how many pictures of beautiful thirteen-year-olds I saw, there was always an even more perfect one out there. And there were pictures of thirteen-year-olds without their suits, which was initially shocking, but it was the same drug in a more potent form, and I needed the more potent form to get the same thrill.

Azov would sell film sets of boys, starting with fully clothed, then "casually" playing on the beach, then the inevitable skinny dipping, and as the years went by, the poses became increasingly sexualized, like wrestling nude. They were not having sex, but they were getting close. Like any mindless lemming I pursued those pictures right off the cliff. And I saw more than just casual nudism; on several sites the children were clearly being abused. No smiling, happy kids but sad ones being hurt, and I was participating in their pain, at times gratified by it. I probably bought more than a hundred DVDs over the course of three to four years. I would breathlessly await receipt, masturbate furiously for a few hours, and throw half of them away, only to buy the same ones again three or four months later.

The abyss spoke to me. My drinking became more frequent and catastrophic. One morning I woke up to find the nail of my left big toe gone; I had avulsed it from my foot while drinking in my rocking chair. I was so intoxicated at the time I had no memory of doing it. I was hung over most mornings. Fran, aware of the drinking if not the porn, started talking about leaving. I would wake up on Sunday morning to go downstairs to clean the wine-stains I had inevitably caused the night before. I was going through a case weekly, putting the empty bottles in multiple trash bins in a pitiful attempt to disguise the extent of my excess from my neighbors.

On one summer weekend, Fran and Bridget were visiting my family back in Georgia. Their presence in the house was at least a mild inhibition to my worst behavior. I was scheduled to join them later that weekend, so had time for one final Friday night spree before flying to Georgia. That night I got so drunk I drove barefoot to a local casino with the confused goal of somehow earning an entry into the World Series of Poker. Someone called the police who found me passed out on the steering wheel of my car. I was booked and jailed overnight. I suppose it would have been humiliating if I could remember any of it. Thankfully, it did not hit the papers.

Fran was relieved because for at least a bit, I got scared and stopped drinking. When sober I could be a good guy, present and less irritable and isolative. Maybe this would be the wakeup call I needed. My driver's license was suspended for six months, until I got a temporary hardship license Fran would have to drive me to work, dropping me at the office with the parting admonition of "make good choices!"

I had not surrendered and was resentful of the entire process. I had made one little mistake, which everyone was blowing out of proportion. If Fran and Bridget loved me so much, why were they always on my case? I stayed sober for six months, went to my classes and paid my fine until I could get my full license back. I sold most of the wine I had collected over that last five years to "prove" I had changed, but it was self-deception. As long as I had a secret sexual life, I would never stay sober. At least now I did realize I drank not to be sophisticated, but because I really liked the oblivion of intoxication, and life felt unendurable without it.

Court had several expectations before I could get my precious driver's license back. I had to go to AA, a program I found perplexing since they required no dues or membership fees. I could not figure out why they were nice to me, since I saw nothing in it for them. But drinking was not the real problem. Maybe I had to give up wine, but the only way you were getting my computer away was by prying it from my cold dead hands.

Any good addict knows about cross addiction. We cut back on drinking but use more pot; our script for oxycodone runs out, and we find ourselves on meth. Anything to not deal with withdrawal or the intrinsic pain of life. Drinking was not my problem. Pornography was dissolving my soul the way acid dissolves flesh. I knew I was hurting kids, and I hated myself for it. I just did not know how to stop. I could stay away from the images for a day, maybe a week, but never longer. And the mornings after were a nightmare. After six months I gladly went back to drinking, knowing I could lose everything, because alcohol was the only relief from self-loathing.

AA did not help since I refused to work the program. I was unwilling to be transparent about my pedophilia. If it killed me, it killed me, but death sounded more attractive than facing my shadow self. A hidden sex addiction is responsible for the treatment failures of thousands of other addicts like me.

I tried desperately to maintain the facade. Late in 2010, I took my wife and daughter to Denver. We stayed in a lovely hotel, the perfect American family. I tried to be a good dad; I have always loved my family more than anything—well, more than anything other than my addictions. But I was tired of life and its contradictions. I only remember fragments of the trip. Getting lost on the way to the hotel. Repeatedly heading down to the bar to buy glasses of pinot noir to drink in bed. Ordering chicken soup from room service. Picking a bone or two out of the soup just before passing out from wine and Ambien. Waking up an hour later gagging on my own blood. I had avulsed my uvula on a chicken bone but did not notice until I almost drowned in blood.

A month later, I went by myself to Manhattan for the annual meeting of the Academy of Child and Adolescent Psychiatry. By day, I was playing the role of hero psychiatrist in a rural state. People were so impressed with what we were doing in Montana with such limited resources. But every night I would get drunk and go watch *Billy Elliot* on Broadway. I loved the play of course. The idea of a boy trying to be a guy but also having an interest in non-stereotypic boy activities, the idea of trying to escape a closeted world, the idea of having an effeminate, potentially gay friend, and having it be okay— these were all my themes, themes that danced in my head daily. But I also loved the beautiful, elegant boys who played the lead. Back in the hotel room I would berate myself as a worthless "pedophile," a word I had never previously uttered out loud.

But dim insight did not keep me from self-destructive rituals.

One day a shocking announcement appeared on the Azov website. Sascha had died. Sascha was their star; they had started filming him as a ten- or eleven-year-old. As always with those movies, they started with casual pictures, then swimsuit issues with his speedos getting smaller while he got bigger. Finally, by the time he was thirteen or fourteen, there were the inevitable nude sauna photos, and all pretense of childhood innocence evaporated.

The post on Azov indicated he was killed in a high speed one vehicle crash. The proprietors of the website were devastated and thanked all Sascha's fans for their support in this difficult time. All his photo sets were 30% off. I do not know whether any of this is true. Maybe the kid got tired of it. Maybe his dad beat up the photographer in Russia. But my guess is it was true. He might have been fifteen or sixteen by then and tens of thousands of images of him nude were posted on the internet, photos that would never, ever go away. Maybe he had a first girlfriend. Maybe she knew. Maybe his family needed more money. Maybe the photographer wanted more sexualized behavior. Maybe he got as drunk as I got. Maybe none of the above happened. All I can visualize is a wreck with shards of glass and a hubcap flung to the side of the road. And in some way, I had contributed to his demise. Of course, I purchased the memorial video, 30% off.

In late January 2011, I was on call for the Youth Partial Hospital, an intensive outpatient service where chronically ill patients could get treatment and schooling during the day but still could go home on nights and weekends. One of my duties as the attending physician was to see all the kids who were secluded, or sometimes restrained, because they were out of control. We prided ourselves in resorting to these strategies as little as possible, but our patients were severely troubled, often self-abusive, and sometimes had to be physically placed in time out until they could calm themselves down.

I was called to see Trevor. He was eleven. He and his two siblings were raised by a vicious biological father who went to jail for beating them. Trevor had been repeatedly locked in the trunk of the car while the parents were at the bar. He had almost frozen to death during one of these episodes. Winter was his worst time.

He had been secluded, which consisted of being locked in a small room with only a small observation window. I am sure it reminded him of being confined by his parents. My only job was to document that he was physically safe. What was unusual this time was that he had taken off all his clothes. He was crouched in the corner, visible only by the side. He talked to me more than he ever had. "They locked me in the trunk. They hated me, everyone hates me. Now you guys are locking me up, just like them!" He stared hitting his head on the wall. We got him underwear and a blanket, we told him he was safe, that we cared about him and would not ever let him be hurt again. Amazingly, he just fell asleep. I think he exhausted himself after three hours of raging.

But all I knew was that, seen nude from the side, he looked just like Sascha.

I felt dazed, like I had been hit with a cement block. I staggered to the staff room in back. The charge nursed asked if I was okay. I wrote the seclusion order, and silently drove home. I was in a living nightmare.

The only thing left for me was divine intervention. It is probably just as well that I did not know it would present itself in the form of US Postal Inspectors.

In early February 2011, just a week or two after I had seen Trevor in seclusion, I received an unusual letter sent from a post office box in Charlotte, NC. It was a printed advertisement for hard core child pornography. There were no pictures, but it promised that in these films the young actors would have "their boyish holes filled." The names of the boys were similar but not identical to the names of the boys on the Azov site. I ripped the ad up, keeping only the envelope. Why did this get sent to me? What they were advertising sounded truly awful. I knew the films I watched and the photo sets I purchased were pornography. They existed to show the boys' bodies off, nothing more, nothing less. But this was flat out rape.

I knew I should just forget about it. It was probably just a trap in some way. But what if kids, kids like Trevor were being horrible harmed, and I did nothing. In some way I cannot explain, the letter felt strangely providential. I was trapped like a wolf in a snare. I could not go on like this, but I despaired of thinking I could ever stop. I had tried so many times, and always came crawling back. When I tell my story, people often ask why I did not talk to a counselor or a religious friend. But how do you tell someone your whole life is a sham and fraud. How? I had this crazed fantasy that maybe I could be a good guy again, save kids instead of contributing to their destruction, and maybe the police would understand, go easy on me. And how could I ask kids like Trevor to be brave when I could not be brave myself? It felt as if everything was moving towards this letter, and I could not wish it away.

I had to do something, and I knew of one person that might help.

A patient's father was an FBI agent in town. I like to think I had really helped his kid. Maybe I could talk with him, get this letter off my mind. When I mentioned the letter to him, he immediately knew what to do; he had a friend in Seattle he could talk to, and they would get in touch with me soon.

Sure enough, I had a phone call in a day or two that a postal inspector agent from Seattle with the curious appellation of T.J.

Westcott wanted to talk. He flew in from Washington to meet with me, a bantam man with a confident air. He would love to discuss the letter and assured me he could do it in a way that would not embarrass me. I had taken a day or two off work and told him I could meet at the downtown post office.

I really did not know what to think. I did not know what Mr. Westcott thought or knew, but on some level I did not care. I left the office where I had worked for seventeen years and never entered it again.

The night before the interview I drank two bottles of Sauvignon Blanc. It was my last drink—I have over eleven years of sobriety as of this writing. The next morning, I drove to the post office after getting a cup of coffee at the adjacent Starbucks. It was a cold, bleak February morning, typical of Billings that time of year. I told the postal clerk I was there to meet Mr. Westcott. He gave me a dead look and told me to wait a minute. Westcott appeared with a sad-eyed partner and took me up to a non-descript office on the second floor. Once there, he assured me that everything, I was doing was voluntary, that I could leave at any time. Of course, most of me knew it was a set-up, but if there was even a one percent chance that somehow, I could be the good guy again, that I could be relieved of my horribly guilty conscience and start over, it would be worth it. I told the inspector about my letter. They were not the slightest bit interested in the letter; they were only interested in me.

If I had received such a letter, it could have only happened because I had solicited information from dubious sources. I think for a minute or two I feigned ignorance, but then Mr. Westcott slipped a sheet of paper with the names and dates of the films I had bought ten years earlier from Award Films, including *You Are Not Alone*. They had a list of everyone who bought films from Award and another list of everyone who bought films from Azov, which had just been busted by Canadian authorities, although I did not know that at the time. Mr. Westcott told me I had a problem, and that I had to admit it. He said he knew all about me, what a great doctor I was, how many nice things he had heard about me, but I had a problem. And maybe, just maybe he could help me.

That really was all I needed. I finally said out loud the words I bitterly cursed myself with for so many years. "I am a pedophile."

Which of course, he already knew. I remember only little bits and pieces of the next hour. I had never been interviewed by the police before in any capacity. They did the "good cop, bad cop" routine which I now recognize as basic police protocol, with Westcott reminding me how much trouble I could be in and the sidekick with the sad eyes telling me that by being open and honest, I was "helping myself out." It went on and on, Westcott explaining to me that he possessed a remarkable gift of being able to "sniff out" pedophiles like a bloodhound and that the postal service sent him all over the country to interview people like me. He knew I wasn't the worst. He didn't understand why we were the way we were, just that we were, and that he was sure he would find child pornography, bestiality, necrophilia, and coprophilia on my computer. They always do. (Sorry, T.J., just the child pornography, but that was enough.)

Westcott asked "Jim, do you have child pornography at home, because if you do, we need to get that out of there." He made it sound as if he was worried about me, and that if we just got that material out of there, it might be okay. But I knew it was done. I was done. I signed an agreement for them to search the house.

While he fetched a white generic SUV (all feds drive white generic SUVs), I asked the other guy who did not look like he was having fun if I was doing the right thing. "Best decision you have made in your life." He was right, but it was also the most painful decision I have ever made in my life.

We drove to my house. Were there guns around? They did not want to be shot. No guns, I replied. I led them to the computer room, showed them the two to three suitcases of videos and photo sets. I gave them everything, all the passwords, credit card receipts for the movies I had bought—everything. I was done, hopelessly done. They were there for two hours alternatively threatening "you do know you could go to prison for this" and encouraging "you are doing a great job, Jim, this is really going to count in your favor. Maybe if you testify against the guys that sold you this stuff, we could all work out a deal." They brought in a photographer that would take pictures of my computer and all the photo CDs and videos, like the picture of confiscated guns and drugs the DEA publicizes. Then they drove me back to the post office, where I waited. They told me they had spoken to my employer; they did not believe I molested children, but they were worried about their "liability" and that they had to let the clinic know about me. Then they told me they had contacted my wife and told her.

Finally, they called Child Services, an agency I had professional contact with daily, because they knew I had a school-aged daughter who might need protection. I asked them if I needed a lawyer (I know, a very dumb question). They demurred, saying they could not give legal advice. Then they gave me their card, said they would be spending the next several weeks going through my computer and media, and said not to turn off my phone in case they had questions. I would hear from them later. I never heard from them again.

The absolute worst moment of my life was going to see Fran.

I pulled her in from patients. She knew I was going to visit the agents. I had showed her the advertisement. But of course, I had never told her that I was a pedophile who enjoyed watching sexualized pictures of children and teenagers. Not really a topic that comes up easily in even the most intimate of relationships. But I told the woman that I loved, the mother of my child, that our marriage had been in some ways a sham, that I was a pedophile, that I viewed and collected child pornography, and that after a prolonged and very public period of shame and humiliation for our entire family, I would be going to prison, perhaps for a very long time.

I wish she would have hit me or screamed at me, but she just gave me a sad forlorn but somehow understanding look. I do not know why she did not leave me; she had every right. I was just about to put my blameless wife through years of hell. She knew it. But she just wanted me to know we would get through this somehow. She did not want details; she just wanted to know what we needed to do to survive. That moment, the single most painful moment of my life, was the moment life began for me again. At that horrible bottom, I saw in her look the light of hope, of someday having a life that was honest, not the superficially cleaned, anesthetized and utterly false self I sold to everyone, particularly myself.

Driving back from the post office, I stopped at another coffee shop to catch my breath before going home. This shop is located two blocks from the building where I worked. I could see the window of my office, an office where I had worked the better part of twenty years. I knew I would never enter that office again, and I never did.

I knew it was going to be bad. If I had known how bad ... it is just as well I did not know how bad.

I just gazed into the window of my office, from the other side, so to speak. I knew that everything I had tried to accomplish in that room was about to come to a catastrophic end, and that I was going to be very sad and very ashamed for a very long time, maybe forever. Maybe everything I had ever tried to accomplish was going to turn to dust.

So, I was surprised that at that horrible moment I had a brief, intense spiritual epiphany, a sense that I finally knew what I was supposed to do with my life and that God was with me, as He had always been, in bed at four, on the rock at camp, even when I was drunk and objectifying His "little ones." In that coffee shop I felt His presence powerfully, for just an instant, and in that instant I knew He would be with me, and it would be okay. Dear reader, if that sounds hokey or contrived, I understand. But that was my sincere experience, and it changed me.

I had always fantasized about what my life should look like. When little, I was going to be an All-Star shortstop for the Cleveland Indians, as a teen I was going to be a famous singer with Julien. The adult me was going to be famous for selflessly helping damaged children by being a kind physician. But those were dream worlds. I had spent thousands of hours listening to adults and children who had been sexually abused, which granted me brief moments where I glimpsed the darkness. But I also knew the other side, the senseless but seemingly irresistible desire, the shame of secrecy and the secrecy of shame. The one thing I do not want to talk about is the one thing I feel compelled to talk about. At that moment I sensed God's true purpose was for me to write this book and to share what little I know in the hope it makes the path easier for those fated to follow.

So Dear Reader, if you have made it this far, please know you have my undying gratitude. You are personally helping me salvage some value out of a life bankrupt and dark, which gives me some comfort as I lament those painful days.

Chapter 12

Burning

For some reason that evening I watched *Gone with the Wind* with Bridget. It was a weeknight. I hardly ever spent time in the evening just hanging out sober with my daughter. I watched Atlanta burn, knowing the flames would soon be headed my way. My head felt swollen and unnatural and my thinking fuzzy. I thought to myself, "oh this is interesting, this is what it feels to be in shock." The detectives warned Fran that thirty percent of the men they investigated for possession of child pornography killed themselves within 72 hours of discovery. To be honest, it was tempting, but I knew it would be just cowardly running away. If a psychiatrist knows anything, it is how painful suicide is for survivors.

Fran, still in shock, dispassionately told me she had talked to the clinic's Chief of Staff, and he wanted to talk with me. She had also gotten the name of a criminal lawyer, and we agreed it would be good to give him a call. She then went alone to bed. Bridget joined her that night. Fran was silent and numb. I tried to sleep downstairs in Bridget's bed, but even with Ambien there would be no sleep for me. Maybe I was paranoid, but all that evening I sensed dark vehicles traversing our isolated cul-de-sac. I would later learn that I had been put on an informal suicide watch by the local police under the recommendation of the federal investigators.

That night I wrote a long letter to Maggie, which after my wife and daughter felt like the most intimate betrayal of all. She would be the one who would have to answer all the questions from patients.

Where is Dr. Peak? Is he sick? Why don't you know when he is going to return? I had to explain that I had a lifelong issue with a sexual attraction to children which I kept secret from everybody in my life. That I had been interviewed by the police. And that I knew I would never return to our practice, leaving her to clean up the excrement in the Aegean stable I left behind.

I wrote a similar letter to Luke and my other colleagues in the department. Already busy to over bursting with their own practices, I knew that it would be their burden to manage my patients in my absence. First by pretending they did not know what was going on, later by having to answer the unanswerable when, why, and how. The letters were surprisingly easy to write. Part of me had been waiting for this moment for so long and I had an idea of what I needed to say. I was so tired of pretending. I listened to Nixon's resignation speech on the radio when I was twelve, and I was so tired of my own Nixonian deceit. I wanted the old me dead. I had little to no expectation that my new life would be worth living but I was done with pretense.

I met the Chief the next day. He wanted my side of the story. I told him I compulsively viewed sexual images involving children, but had never abused a child, or taken advantage of my patients in any way. He told me the clinic knew I was a good doctor and wanted me to get the help I needed to be a good doctor again. Frankly, I had not expected to hear that from him, and we agreed to meet the next day to make further plans.

That first meeting was just the Chief of Staff and me. The next meeting was less intimate and congenial. Risk management personnel were present in force. The Chief had spoken to his boss, the CEO, and since our previous conversation they had become convinced it would be best for me to immediately resign and he just happened to have the paperwork conveniently available. Empathy had been replaced by pragmaticism. Whatever I had accomplished in seventeen years was erased in about seventeen hours. I never officially heard from the clinic again. I had transformed from valued doctor to a public relations nightmare.

As I left the hospital for the last time, the Chief told me I might want to contact Mike Ramirez, who worked with impaired physicians through an organization called the Montana Professional Assistance Program (MPAP). Mike was an energetic, athletic man and a pioneer in the field. Through his leadership, Montana possessed one of the best professional assistance programs in the country, despite having limited staff and budget.

At this point I was a catastrophe. My job was my whole identity. There were so many things to mourn; betraying my family, abandoning my patients and colleagues, and ultimately going to jail were all on the list. But honesty compels me to admit the worst part was having to shed the false mask my job and societal position provided. I could never be the "good guy" again, and I thought that would kill me. I was naked to the world, and it was not a pretty sight.

I had never heard of MPAP. Professional assistance programs exist in most states, and act as an intermediary between licensed professionals and professional disciplinary boards. They have the delicate responsibility of balancing treatment to medical personnel while protecting the public from impaired practitioners. Like many people in this field, Mike was a former alcoholic, well acquainted with the dark night of the soul and the inconsolable bewilderment of despair. I had never breathed a word about my sexual attraction to anyone before talking to the police. I cannot recommend coming out to the authorities. But my secret had burdened my soul for so long that at this point I truly had nothing to lose, and I was almost compelled to inflict the story on others.

I basically fell in a heap on Mike's floor and told my story as best I could. As a psychiatrist, I knew I should not kill myself. Suicide would solve my problem, but no one else's. For decades I had told my patients that their lives had meaning, their pain was real, but not insurmountable, and that life got better, but only if you were patient and willing to work. No matter how bad things feel, your life has meaning, and is intimately connected to the lives of others, whether you like it or not. You may have a horrible illness like schizophrenia that torments you daily and makes it hard to have the life you dreamed of, the one that seems so effortless to everybody else, but I care about you, other people care about you, and you can piece together a life worth living despite painful memories, and heartbreaking sadness.

When I told that to kids who lost their parents to murder or drugs, to teenagers thrown out of their families for being gay, or to adults in the ICU after yet another overdose, did I mean it, or was it just a line? If I meant it I needed to live it. But I was done lying. I was done wearing the façade of the good guy. I was not the hero. I was the villain. I told Mike I was a pedophile who had watched child pornography on and off for four years, drank two bottles of wine daily, hated himself, and saw nothing redeeming in his life or story. I needed help with how to survive so I did not abandon a family that deserved so much better.

Mike listened seriously and sincerely, finally saying "Yeah, what a catastrophe. But you are in the right place, and your Higher Power loves you." It is amazing how healing it is for someone to listen to your story without judgement. He did not turn to stone when I told him about my loathed attractions. He knew things were bad. But this is not the first time he had heard bad. And the naked soul is the teachable soul. As horrible and as hopeless as I felt, it was in Mike's office that I was gifted the first glimpse of a life worth living.

It may sound ridiculous that as a psychiatrist I thought I was beyond help, but no one talked about problems like mine. Therapists hear a lot about sexually and physically abusive men and the trauma and destruction they inflict on the young and innocent, but rarely work with the man themselves. In much of therapy, offenders dead and alive haunt the treatment, the unpresent presence thought to be only addressed through the correctional system.

But Mike saw otherwise. He knew that I was not a contact offender, that I had a compulsive behavior with addictive traits, and that there was hope for me. But I needed a lot of help, and I needed it fast or I would drown in despair. And I was so thirsty for wine and porn. The only thing that I knew would help me stop thinking about wine and porn was wine and porn. My body ached for it. Mike said he had to make a few calls but would be in touch with me tomorrow, that suicide was unacceptable and to hang on no matter what.

I spent the next hour and a half trying to find my car. I was so internally preoccupied I had no recollection of where I had parked it.

The next day I met with my attorney Jay Lansing. I had been given Jay's name by the clinic, the last direct contact I would have with them. Jay was very busy and hesitant to take my case, but I begged, and finally wore him down. He had an office on the twelfth floor of the Wells Fargo Building with an incredible view of the eastern Montana prairies. Whenever I visited with Jay to go over my criminal case, I would just imagine how nice it would be to jump off the building into oblivion.

Jay is a proud Iowa Hawkeye, a Hemingway devotee, and a good man. He is also a clear-eyed realist, which I needed, even if I did not like it. I quickly learned that in federal court leverage for the defense is very limited, and the prosecuting attorney assigned to my case had staked her reputation on aggressively prosecuting cases like mine. She had just appeared on the cover of a local women's magazine portrayed as a vigilant protector of women and children. The issue was prominently displayed on the coffee table in Jay's waiting room. Her office was unlikely to negotiate much. We just had to wait and see. I had not been charged yet, but they were reviewing evidence.

He also had a letter on his desk from a client that had committed suicide prior to being charged and he told me that if I was to work with him, I had to promise not to become another dead client. I thought only psychiatrists worried about suicidal clients, but I was wrong. I had serious charges and was prominent in the community. It was going to get very ugly, but he was going to defend me to the best of his ability and attempt to negotiate the minimal term of incarceration. My job was to neither get too up or too down, and live one day at a time.

I drove home to find my wife furiously chopping vegetables for a salad. The shock had worn off, and she was justifiably horrified, shamed, and betrayed. "How could you do this to me, to us, what am I supposed to tell our daughter? You know Child Protective talked to Bridget at school, wanting to know whether you are molesting her. I get to meet with them tomorrow. They want to know if we need a safe house." Fran who never swore, went on. "This is a nightmare, just a fucking nightmare. How can this be happening; this cannot be happening." She then broke down hysterically sobbing in a way I have never seen before. The intensity of her despair was overwhelming. Snot was leaking from her nose. "I am dying, there is a cancer in my heart. Jimmy, how could you do this to a family that loved you so much. Go."

I stumbled out the door and started walking aimlessly, astonished that I could have so thoroughly destroyed my life in such a short time, still trying to figure how who sent the ad, and why, still incapable of recognizing what was in front of my nose. Two hours later I finally realized that the ad was a fabrication, sent by the postal inspectors to individuals on their radar and that any response triggered an investigation. And I had believed I could be the hero again. Fool. Fran and Bridget. My poor patients and their families, my colleagues. What a catastrophe. I finally came home to a wife who pretended I was not there and took a shower. The shower is an excellent place to cry.

Morning came, fresh and hopeful as ever, mocking my sense of eternal night, and Mike reminded me that I all I had to do was the next right thing and that God would provide. I was desperate to do anything that might limit the damage to my wife and daughter, no matter how humiliating or humbling. Mike gave me the names of several facilities that might be willing to work with me. As bleak as things were, looking back I was lucky. I had resources to afford treatment and already some folks who were willing to help, even though I feared I was beyond redemption. I started calling treatment facilities. It is not an easy situation to explain to strangers on the phone. Not everybody wanted to consider sex addicts; even fancy medical centers like Menninger were wary.

I had to get out of Billings, with its constant reminders of failure, or I was going to die drinking. There was a facility just north of Dallas in Argyle, Texas called the Santé Center for Healing that was willing to work with me and had Mike's blessing. I arrived in Texas within a week of going to the post office.

For all my faults, I possessed the one trait required to be successful in treatment. I was all in. I could not visualize the road ahead, but I knew I could not go back the way I came. And since my cover was blown, there was no reason to hold back. This is it; if I am an untreatable monster, so be it, but I cannot be the old me. My patients inspired me; they had been willing to talk about trauma and shame and addiction. Who was I not to learn from their bravery?

Those three months saved my life. Santé was an unpretentious facility on a beautiful country hilltop. There were fifty or sixty residents at any one time. I had several interviews the first day, some more pleasant than others. Pedophiles creep people out, even clinicians. I arrived on a Sunday, and the last event before bed was a community meeting facilitated by patients who were almost done with the program. No staff. I was asked at the end to introduce myself. Do I act like I did at AA the first time and just tell them the bare minimum? Can non-professionals see me as a deeply flawed human or am I a hopeless monster?

"My name is Jim Peak. I am a child psychiatrist from Montana who has had a life-long sexual attraction to children which I never told anyone about. I have been investigated by federal police for viewing child pornography and will probably be sent to prison. I drink nightly. I have a wife and a child. I have not directly harmed children, but I have horrible thoughts and have seen horrible things and am trying to figure out whether there is any future for me."

I just stared at the linoleum flooring trying to find patterns and symmetries in the unobtrusive design, if only to distract myself and avoid eye contact. Absolute silence. I was certain there was several people in that room who had been molested as a child. I was not sure whether they would be able to see me for myself or as the person that most reminded them of their abuser. I knew I was going to wear the label of sex offender until I died. Would that define me? I was terrified no one would be able to see beyond that. The chairperson closed the meeting, and I went alone to my room. But no one yelled at me, no one spit on me, which I was grateful for. One day at a time, do not focus on the future, just focus on today, being sober, and being vulnerable.

I am so grateful to Santé; it was the first time I felt truly human since I was ten. No one is in treatment because life is going well.

Everyone was ashamed, everyone had secrets. Santé was a pioneer in working with patients with sexual compulsions, and there were nightly twelve-step meetings for sex addicts that always had ten or twelve participants, including several women. I was not as terminally unique as I thought.

Santé treated it all. Desperate alcoholics and pill fiends. Dangerously fragile anorexics. There was an 18-year-old kid caught having sex with his dog, a 24-year-old tennis instructor who kept having affairs with her adolescent students, and so many people caught in the web of prostitution, meaningless hook-ups, and pornography. I was not even the only one with serious legal charges hanging over my head. And I was finally not drunk. The buzzing in my ears stopped, my tongue was no longer blackened and burned from wine tannins. I got some sleep.

But what a swathe of destruction I had inflicted. And all those years of lying to myself, to my family, to the world. I had been so selfish, so careless with the hearts of the people I ostensibly loved. How do you live with that?

My first meeting the next day was with Sam Hill who would be my primary therapist. He was the definitive Texan, stocky with light blue eyes, a crimson Texas Aggies polo shirt, and a handlebar moustache. He would have made a great stand-in for the sheriff in *Butch Cassidy*. He radiated presence and authenticity. The facility is located on the highest hill in Denton County. Legend has it Sam was struck twice by lightening on that hill. The storms subsided, yet Sam abided. He had already talked with Mike Ramirez, shook my hand firmly, and said, "Jim, your life is going to change, because Mike tells me you will do the work. I have something for you to read." I thought it would be an AA book, but it was the *Meditations* by Marcus Aurelius, the great Roman Stoic. I treasure that book, both for its wisdom, and as a symbolic connection to great teachers.

Jess Montgomery was my wonderful psychiatrist. Stepping into his office was like looking in the mirror of my own abandoned domain back in Montana. He was a tall, dignified man with a calming presence. He was very skilled in finding compelling metaphors for addiction in children's books like *The Velveteen Rabbit* and recognized the compulsive nature of sexual obsession. He empathized with the marginalized and misbegotten without condescension. He knew I broke a taboo, but if I could persevere, my higher power would provide. This was a bit too ethereal to me at the time, but I could not argue with the fact that my best thinking got me in treatment, and I needed to have faith in the process, faith that I was where I needed to be. It reminded me of my recent goodbye to Bridget before getting on the plane to Dallas. I was trying to figure out what to say. She just started singing "Let It Go" from *Frozen* before giving me a hug. I had forgotten how good my life was; Santé gave me the time and space to remember.

Without the usual crutches, everyone was on edge. Coffee had to be strictly quarantined. Furtive smoking was omnipresent. People would do anything to get high. It was not jail, there was always contraband available, and desperation inspires creativity. My first roommate calmly watched as his belongings were searched, comforted by the fact he had a fifth of vodka taped to his calf. Clients passed out from smuggled pills. Couples disappeared into the woods to have sex after having known each other for less than two hours. As a group we had spent years in denial of our illness, and were desperate for a fix, any fix. Less than half of the people who started were able to finish. "Walk-offs" were common. It was a four-mile hike to the closest place to buy beer, but people made the trek every weekend.

I stayed put. Fran, Bridget, and pending federal charges clarified my mind regarding the stakes of sobriety.

I did well in treatment because I was truly desperate. I had nothing to lose, no reservations about sobriety. One of my first "therapeutic activities" was on the ropes course and involved the "Tower of Surrender." This required the participant to climb a vertical pole forty feet high while suspended in a harness hooked to a series of cables. Basically, it was bungee jumping. Generally, I do not bungee jump, because as you will recall from my *Thrillseeker* days I am an enthusiastic fan of body integrity. I like handrails, staying far away from the edge, and fastening my seatbelt until the aircraft has come to a full and complete stop and the cabin door has been depressurized. So, when Sam requested a volunteer, no one was more surprised than I was to see my hand raised in mid-air. Several people had gone up the pole, only to lose their nerve and come back to ground. But uncharacteristically, I swan-dived into the ether.

My life of safe conformity and fear were over. I would fly or die in the effort.

Chapter 13

Unmasking

Gratitude. The one thing I never wanted to happen did happen. The future would be filled with difficulties, yet during those first days at Santé I felt lighter than I had in years. Veterans called it "the pink cloud." I was no longer trapped in the futile and exhausting cycle of work for ten hours, go home, get drunk, watch porn; repeat.

For twenty years my working life had consisted of moving from patient to patient fifteen times a day. All problems, no matter how severe, had to be addressed in a thirty-minute time slot. I knew what I would be doing and who I would be seeing eight months in advance. Now I was shipwrecked, and imagined hungry sharks everywhere.

I no longer woke up with my ears ringing, my head buzzing, and my tongue burning. Those sensations had been with me so long, I thought they were normal. Now I had time. I was terrified of time. Without someone else's immediate crisis in front of me, I had no choice but to reflect on my own.

Sam's office was in an attic loft, filled with Texas Aggie paraphernalia as well as several tender pictures of Johnny, his teenage son afflicted with Down's Syndrome. He cantilevered his cowboy boots on a footstool, leaned back, took a hard look at me with those light blue eyes and said, "start at the beginning."

"I am a sick, evil person whose life is a lie and who deserves prison."

Sam could be an intimidating presence. In his previous existence, he had fought in the parking lot of most every honky-tonk in Brazos County. So he caught my attention when he instantly snapped out of his comfortable position, opened those blue eyes wide and quietly but clearly stated; "Cow dung. Do not waste our time together. I have no interest in your unhelpful flawed self-opinion. I want to know how we got here."

"It is a long sad story," I replied.

"It always is," he said as he again leaned back.

Over the next two weeks I pieced it together as best I could.

How alone and different I had always felt. How ashamed, guilt ridden and sick of it all. My life presented as a comfortable suburban house, but the foundation was unstable and once you peeled off the wallpaper black mold was everywhere.

"Sam, I have fooled everyone into thinking I am such a good guy, but I am not; after work, all I do is walk around, dream about my stupid fantasy band, and try not to think too much about boys, until I get drunk and then that is all I want to think about."

"I love children. I love my patients. I want nothing but good for them. It is the reason I wake up in the morning. And then at night—it is like I am no longer human."

Sam took a big gulp from his bottomless mug of coffee and sighed. "Jim, what makes you think you are so damn unique. Saying one thing while doing another is an essential human survival skill for all of us, but you in particular; you learned it repeatedly from an early age. It kept you alive. It got you through school and work and marriage. But the price is high, and God thinks you cannot afford to pay it anymore. So here we are. Your pain is good, don't run away or deny it, and do not waste it all on self-pity; without change tears are just salty water. Remember this pain, treasure it always. None of us is as good as we think we are, or as bad as we think we are, not even you."

"But prison!"

"What about it."

"I can't handle prison."

"More cow dung! You don't even know if you are going. And if you do, prison will be a piece of cake after the last few years. Weak people think they are tough. Tough people think they are weak. You're pretty tough, or you wouldn't be here."

I told him about camp, the years of lying and deception about the things I had seen that I loved and despised. He knew those behaviors were bad for me and bad for the universe, but on hearing them he did not turn to stone. And I told him that as bad as I felt about the pornography, that I felt worse about leaving my patients. I thought of all my foster kids, the Lenzis. I was abandoning the abandoned, worsening their trauma instead of alleviating it. Everyone else at Upstate took the Hippocratic Oath; I apparently substituted the Hypocritic one.

I told him I could not stop crying. I had not dared allow myself to shed tears since camp all those years ago. Now it felt as if they would never stop. I would have to get up in the middle of lunch or group, overwhelmed with self-hatred and fear, and go sob in the toilet. I was terrified I would spend the rest of my life a sad, shamed husk.

"Jim, your pride makes you think you are special, but you are not, you are just another sex addict. You guys are everywhere but no one wants to face it because it is so shaming. The average guy makes an Anthony Weiner joke while praying his wife doesn't know how to access his computer's search history, but for any addict of any type—you, me, or the other guy— where we go, pain and chaos inevitably follow. The question is, do we have the guts to accept who we are, and to do anything and everything, whatever it takes, to change and make amends, so we can live the life of solemn dignity God wants for us? Being attracted to children creeps other people out, but it doesn't creep God out. He made you that way; you must figure out how to live with it without hurting yourself and the people you love. An addict is someone who engages in compulsive self-destructive behavior. That we can work with, if— and this is a huge if—if you are tired of lying. If you are, this catastrophe was both inevitable and the best thing that ever happened to you—you just don't know it yet. If you are not tired of lying, there is plenty more pain where that came from."

Part of me thought Sam was nuts or naïve, but he radiated truth and authenticity like the noonday sun. Whenever I tried to use my clever monkey brain to argue with him, he responded the same way: "Jim, you are a smart guy, a really smart guy," which made the good little boy within beam, only for him to raise his voice slightly to remind me "and that is of no assistance to you whatsoever. Your best thinking got you here. Less thinking, more listening, more accepting."

I was surprised to find that at Santé I was not as obsessed with sex. I had never really appreciated the connection between alcohol and pornography and the extent to which each supported the other. It wasn't as if I changed or became something different, but somehow the fact that it was no longer solely my secret allowed some of its allure to seep away.

Initially I was only allowed two ten-minute phone calls a week. I talked to Fran three days after my admission. After asking about my well-being, she let me know she was doing a lot of thinking. Friends had offered her advice, telling her that she needed to escape, from me, from Billings, from the inevitable fallout. "Jimmy, I love you, and want to be there, but it is so hard. Why should Bridget have to deal with this? She is just twelve, how is she supposed to face this? Maybe if the two of us moved to Wyoming we could start over. I hate to leave you when it is so hard for you, but I must think of Bridget first. And I don't know if I can ever trust you again."

I had no response. It was the nightmare scenario, the nuclear warhead I did not know how to disarm. I get exposed, arrested, and disgraced. My family and friends abandon me. And life as I know it is over.

And it was 100% completely on me. No one else to blame. If Fran was not considering this option, she would be crazy. That she could empathize with my position even though I had put her in an untenable position just made me feel even more of a cad.

For inscrutable architectural reasons Santé's phone bank was located next to a tiny but well-loved indoor swimming pool. Hordes of patients would stand by the pool waiting for their allotted ten minutes, and my session was close to expiring. How do I handle the most difficult phone conversation of my life in five minutes, while avoiding splashing water?

"Fran, I am attracted to young boys and teens. I have watched a lot of child pornography. That is why I am so miserable. That is why I drink. Nothing else is there, but I know that is enough. You must protect Bridget, and I know you have to do what you have to do. And whatever you need to do I will support the best I can." While I was speaking a multi-colored inflatable ball struck me in the face; I said good-bye and hung up.

This was not going to just blow up on me, who had planted the explosive and set the timer; it was going to blow up on the people I most loved and cared about. Sam, as always, was right when he reminded me that "Sometimes addicts hurt strangers, but mainly we hurt the ones we love."

It was spring in Texas Hill Country. Azaleas were blooming. The chill of winter was fading. In the pond by the walking path, newly hatched ducklings were taking their brave first swim following their proud, vigilant parents, tracking them so closely they might have been magnetized. Hawks flew in effortless lazy circles overhead. The ceaseless cycle of life carried on all around me, mocking my despair.

I started grasping at straws, praying that the feds would take pity on me and reconsider prosecution. On a later phone call, Jay had to sadly disabuse me of such hopes. Not only were they highly motivated to proceed, but the prosecuting attorney had already formally notified the Montana Board of Medical Examiners that I was going to be charged with possession of child pornography, and the Board immediately and indefinitely suspended my medical license. I faced up to ten years in prison, depending on what charge the government chose to pursue, and there was little to nothing he could do about it.

But there are two magical things that can occur in treatment which make the unendurable endurable. First, you are surrounded by people with unique circumstances but similar problems. Nobody came because they needed a stress-free vacation. We were all addicts who lied to the ones we loved, selfishly, carelessly.

Second, you get a chance to take off that sticky, unconvincing mask, maybe for the first time since childhood.

Most of us spend much of our lives focused on meaningless ephemera. The day-to-day routine of feeding the kids, fulfilling customer orders, repairing the fence. But in our psyches lie deeper darker waters. Those can be childhood wounds, un-mourned losses, half-treated mental illnesses, or any of the seven deadly sins. And when we find a substance or a behavior that can make those aching feelings fade, replaced by an unearned but very palpable sense of euphoric power and vigor, resistance crumbles.

But intoxication is a transient, albeit charming lie. Whether it is drugs, sex, power, or money, there is never enough of it; no thrill lasts long enough, much less forever. But this is a familiar story. The miracle of treatment is that when you put a bunch of burned-out, phony, self-absorbed, and self-deluded drunks, druggies, and sex addicts together and make them talk about what is real, defenses drop and things can change. Feelings do not last. Euphoria does not last. But neither does despair. People do crazy things to themselves and others because they hurt so much. Treatment is not just your chance to get clean; it is your chance to *come* clean. If you have a biological child you never told your spouse about, here is your chance to acknowledge it. If you got drunk at sixteen and had sex with your cousin, this is where you look at the mirror. If you have been embezzling from your company for the last three years, welcome home.

I am not saying everyone has a *Dateline* type of secret, although there are plenty of them, but everyone has thoughts and behaviors and beliefs that shame and motivate. The beautiful curvy woman whose family always told her no man would marry a fat girl, begins using diet pills for "energy" and to lose weight. One year later she is physically gaunt and hopelessly addicted. Santé is where you go when you finally give up on running away.

I never heard a story in treatment I could not relate to. In group, seated on my left is a grizzled, blurry-eyed eighty-year-old former Florida legislator whose family connections had controlled a rural county for generations, but whose arrogance and hard drinking had alienated both his family and his constituents, leaving him powerless, alone, and vulnerable for the first time. On my right is a handsome, cocky rodeo bronc rider, barely twenty, fighting off hordes of women and photographers, but already taking Vicodin for pain and amphetamine for hangovers. He was ten when he watched his sister drown in a sneaker wave off the Hawaiian coast. Now he has one baby in tow, and another on the way, of course with different mothers. The high school teacher fired for making a drunken pass at one of his students. The school bus driver who just got her second DWI, this time on the job.

Domestic violence and bitter divorces. Crappy jobs, bratty kids, boring lives. So many reasons to flee reality. But when you slow people down, and sober them up, the suffering unhappy human re-emerges, doing the best they can in a confusing world. We told each other our stories, and if they could make sense to our fellows, maybe they could start to make sense to us. Empathy for the human experience is the miracle ingredient. We all suffer; the only way to diminish it is to face it. We had all postponed the confrontation with our pain, pretending that if we ignored it long enough, it would leave us alone, when in fact it just spreads like contagion, infecting all our closest contacts. But if you just stop, turn away from the pulsing glare of your fake life, and be authentic, you might be amazed.

Yes, there are the sharp outlines of your failures, which you have tried to minimize or deny for so long, but if you look long enough and carefully enough you might also see the hazy outline of a simpler, more honest future, and perhaps, a glimpse of the eternal. Such epiphanies do not last—reality and fear always come cascading back. But realizing, if only for an instant, there is something other than enslavement and despair, and that all of us, no matter how defeated, always carry the pilot light of the soul deep within: this is the seed of rebirth. This simple knowledge can inspire the courage necessary to keep moving forward, ignorant of where we are going but certain it is better than where we have been.

I was mandated to attend Caduceus in Fort Worth, a twelve-step meeting for medical professionals. I doubted I would ever practice as a physician again and politely inquired with Sam as to whether a Future Felons of America program was available as an alternative.

The meetings were held in the Tarrant County Medical Association building downtown. About fifty health professionals were there— more than I expected, but I always underestimate how many of us are out there.

The "good doctor" was my beloved persona. Letting it go and revealing the sorry creature underneath was like spilling acid on a sunburn. Nothing mattered more than what others thought of me.

The dreaded introduction, short if decidedly un-sweet. "My name is Jim Peak. I am a child psychiatrist from Billings, Montana. I am an alcoholic who is being investigated for possession of illegal pornography." No making eye contact. Pretend you are somewhere else, maybe sailing on a calm lake. Dr. Forbes was the chairperson, sporting a trim goatee and a tasteful polka-dotted bowtie, radiating serene authority. "You must like kiddie porn," he bellowed. Mortified, I acknowledged in the affirmative. "Well, that is unfortunate. I am sorry about that. We had someone out of Plano way with that little issue. I think she is doing better now, working in an ER somewhere." Could have been worse. Other people introduced themselves. There was the plastic surgeon who wore a baseball cap emblazoned with the letters "DEA" in an ironic reference to the SWAT team that had stormed his office one Monday morning as if it was a cartel laboratory, forever immortalizing him as "DEA Dave." He had been lucky not to be shot.

There were many stories of weak and vulnerable human beings getting hooked one way or another, only to find themselves in a morass of legal and financial catastrophe. What was helpful to me about Caduceus was that the stories had beginnings, middles, and at least sometimes an end. Other people had been where I was standing—they endured, and so could I. Dr. Forbes reassured me that this would all look very different five years down the line. Most of them had been to Santé and referred to it like a fondly remembered boarding school.

And I finally had a chance to think about my life. I wrote to my parents and brothers, and I explained that I was not the son or person they thought I was. All were shocked, some were devastated. I never spoke to my father again. Mom wrote back saying she felt bad for me, but hoped we never had to discuss such awful things again. One brother was supportive. The other, with two little kids at home, could not believe I had been unable to get help. A few of my colleagues from work wrote, one baked cookies. There were people I had seen every working day for fifteen years that I never spoke to again; there were people I thought were just casual acquaintances who went out of their way to contact me and reassure me that I was a good person and a good doctor and that they were hurting for me. In dark days, you find out who your real friends are.

Sex addicts are different, even in treatment. Each Sunday was family visiting day for everyone but those with sexual addictions. We were segregated from the rest of the patients to a building on the campus periphery "for our own protection" to prevent any allegation of untoward behavior towards children or other family member. I called our building "The Island of Lost Boys."

I had to prepare for court. I was asked to do a lot of testing. One of the more unpleasant things was the penile plethysmograph. That is where they put a cuff around your penis to measure your arousal to sexualized pictures of adults and children, under both violent and non-violent circumstances. Not a great way to spend the day, but the results were exactly what I told them. I am attracted to boys 10-14, then girls 10-14, and not much for adults of any age. I was not pretending anymore. I am what I am. Even more important was the polygraph. I admitted to my struggle with pornography but swore I had not directly molested children. But the prosecutors and the court wanted more objective information. Most people assume all pedophiles molest children. I am not sure I understand or even trust polygraphs, but the police and treatment love them. Other clients at Santé were going through the same drill and failed their polygraphs left and right, and I was terrified. I had to work hard to make sure the questions asked were clear. The only acceptable responses are "yes" or "no." Had I ever sexual molested a child? Had I been unprofessional with patients? Had I told the complete truth in treatment? These were the questions they asked.

Of course, the entire procedure is unpleasant. Blood pressure cuffs around your arms and chest. Electrodes on your fingers, machine scratching out graphs in the background. It looks somewhat like an electric chair, although you are not tied down. It is very formal, very scary, and very uncomfortable. It is also a powerful metaphor that the world does not trust you and thinks you are dangerous.

I jumped for joy when I learned I passed it. It meant so much to me that Sam, Dr. Montgomery, and the rest of the team that had been so patient and understanding knew that I was done lying.

Gratitude. I no longer had to wake up asking myself, what did I do last night? No daily headaches. I did not have to delete horrible things from my computer or hide videos. If I thought too much about the future I became frozen, but if I took it one day at a time, things mysteriously seemed to work out better than I could have hoped, just like Sam prophesized.

Because I am selfish and self-centered, I was singularly focused on legalities. If I had been wiser, I would have realized that the critical verdict, and the hinge on which my future balanced was not up to the court, but solely up to Fran. And one of the last stages before you go home is for family to visit for an on-site five-day family support intervention.

I had never gone a week without seeing either Fran or Bridget, so my relief when they were finally escorted into the visiting area was overpowering. I received and gave the two longest hugs of my life.

We met for just an hour or two on the Sunday afternoon they arrived. Bridget in her bright red wool winter coat, bright eyes happy to see me, upbeat as always. Aside from my joy in seeing her I was struck with how she was now having to play the role of good girl living with an alcoholic father, whereas a generation before I had played that role. We transform into what we fear slowly, insidiously. Fran wore black leggings and a casual yellow oxford shirt. After our five-minute hug, she looked at me, then said "Well Peak, you always said we should have more family vacation time, but I wish you would let me pick the destination next time." I only had an hour or two with them before they went back to the hotel. Tomorrow we would talk about how to venture forth together or not into a scary future. That first day Fran spent most of her time talking with Sam while I did puzzles with Bridget and asked about school. When Fran came back into the room her eyes were puffy from crying. I knew it had been a hard interview. Sam called her a cab back to the hotel and we agreed to meet again the next day.

Morbid thoughts churned throughout my restless sleep. Had Fran told Sam she could not handle it anymore and wanted out? She is not a vengeful person but had every right to be disgusted and done.

My shame felt incapacitating. Wisely, I had been practicing what I wanted to say to Bridget and Fran for a week in group, I had to be able to get the words out and make sure this week was more about them than me.

"Bridget, I need to explain to you why I am in treatment. I have a couple of problems. First. I think maybe I drink too much."

Sam was there and reminded Bridget that this was her time to be honest, and she did not have to just be the good little girl.

"Dad, you just 'think' that?"

"Well baby, I know that maybe it has been getting a bit out of hand the last year or two."

"Last year or two? Dad, I have been praying to God for you to quit drinking since I was in kindergarten."

I did not expect that. I thought I had been cleverer. My dad drank in front of us every night for twenty years and generally went to bed trashed. I thought I was doing most of my drinking after Bridget went to sleep. She wouldn't even know I was doing it. Fool. I almost never said a harsh word to the daughter I loved so much; she never merited a harsh word. And I had never received harsh words before, until today. "You never apologize. You drink way too much, way too often, and then you start bumbling around like an idiot. It happens every weekend, it makes me sad and disgusted. Mom and I are tired of it."

I hadn't even gotten to the sex part. I was mortified of my attractions and my internet crimes, but I thought drinking was not that big a deal. I didn't yell when I drank, or hit anyone; I just became sloppy and sentimental, things I hated when I saw it in my dad, but somehow I thought I was different. Bridget disabused me of that belief.

What a terrific child psychiatrist I was. Trying to help others while not being present with the ones I owed the most. Putting my family's lives on autopilot while I did whatever I wanted; how indescribably selfish and blind. The addict part of me had been feeling very sorry for myself and resentful towards the deceptive detectives, when I needed to be grateful and recognize them for what they were, instruments of grace—a last rope to snatch before being sucked into the depths.

Surprisingly, shockingly, Bridget was less upset about my attractions, but maybe she did not fully understand the implications, or maybe times were changing. She was in seventh grade at the time; some of my peers thought I should not talk about my pedophilic attractions with her, that it would be too upsetting and confusing. But I knew I was likely going to prison for it, and that it was going to be in the papers. Believing I could protect her from the consequences of my behaviors would be naïve and unhelpful on my part. Initially I tried to make a joke. You know how you kind of think the boys in Hanson are cute? I sort of thing the boys in Hanson are cute. Went over like a lead balloon. There is very limited humor in these circumstances. So I just said I was attracted to kids. I had never molested anyone and tried hard to be kind and protective at work, but at night when I drank too much (yes, Bridget, I always drank too much) I would get on the computer and look at pictures of children not wearing clothes.

There is nothing like sex addiction to make you say the things you never want to say and do the things you never want to do, and to always remind you that you are made of clay. Later you realize there are specks of iron and diamond mixed in every pile of dirt, even yours, but it sure does not feel that way at the time. She knew about my films of course; there were no secrets in my house growing up, why should I have thought there would be secrets in the house of my adult self? Such are our predictable illusions. But even if she was angry at me, she also loved me, and wanted a healthier more available father. I almost felt like Scrooge in the *Christmas Carol* when the last ghost is gone and it is Christmas and Tiny Tim is not dead yet, and the worst future is not inevitable, but can be changed by changing, I had a chance to actively prove my love and devotion by a willingness to submit to what I knew would be a period of chastening and humility, but that was an insignificant price for a future focused more on others and less on my false self.

The next day we met with a different therapist; someone I had not met before. Her role was to facilitate these two- or three-day intensive family interventions. There were no expectations anything could be resolved in such a brief period. The goal was to get issues on the table, institute a short-term safety plan, and prepare for the harder, long-term work back in Billings. Sam had tried to help me with some of the dirty work. By that I mean he listened to Fran, empathized with her difficult, undeserved choices, but could also vouch that I was way down there, in my heart of hearts, a flawed, but at least semi-decent guy who loved her and our daughter. My behaviors were not a "mistake," and she could expect behavior to change, but not my essential nature. "Jim, I'm not an idiot, it's okay if you are gay. I get it, it's okay, but the kid stuff, why that? Are you sure you weren't abused or something, maybe something you cannot even remember?"

"Well Frannie, I don't think so. I think this is the way I landed when I fell out of the nest. I wish I was normal, but I am not. This is what I find myself thinking about, every day. I try to ignore these thoughts and swear that I will, that I can control how I think and what I do, and I can for a while, and then always I fail, and then it just feels so hopeless ... I don't know, maybe this is what evil looks like." "Peak, stop trying to make me feel sorry for you, I would never have married you if you were evil. Fucked up, that seems likely, but I know you are a good guy, and Bridget loves you so much, even if she is angry and embarrassed." She turned to Sam "So where do we go from here?"

That was when I knew she was going to stay with me, and I felt such relief and gratitude. I hate those press conferences where the wife of the disgraced politician is forced to endure the silent humiliation of "standing by her man," and I had put my innocent wife in that excruciating situation. Every day I remind myself I can never do that to her again, realizing I am always capable of it, if I do not respect the importance of working a program.

A few weeks later, I was all done. I had been there thirteen weeks, attended dozens of meetings, filled up three yellow legal pads with all those thoughts, actions, and memories I had tried so hard to ignore. I had finally been transparent with a few people, and they had not recoiled in horror, but saw me as just another flawed, broken person. In Sam I had a glimpse of the father I dreamed my dad would have been if he could have been.

It was going to be a lot harder back in Billings. Could I avoid liquor stores? The feds had taken my computer, but could I stay away from inappropriate things on my cell phone? How would I deal with the publicity and the legal stress? I was very scared to leave the Santé cocoon, but it was time to pay the piper and build a modest but genuine foundation for my future.

Addicts talk about "God things" because sometimes we feel so fortunate that only God could have arranged such fortuitous outcomes. I am not sure I believe in a God that is pulling strings from behind the curtain but sometimes I am amazed at how things work out.

The first thing I did upon arriving in Billings was find the nearest AA meeting. I knew a relapse was patiently waiting for me and that the next few months would probably determine my long-term future. Drinking and porn were always the way I dealt with sadness and anxiety. And there was a lot of sadness and anxiety in my life. The meeting was at a small church a couple of blocks from my house, a church I had passed by hundreds of times without noticing. I got there on a Thursday at 5:00 just wanting to find the schedule. Serendipitously it turned out there was a meeting in fifteen minutes. I must have had that frightened rabbit look. A toned man with sunglasses got out of a very sharp black and red Corvette and asked me if I needed something, and less than sixty seconds into my first meeting in Billings I met Mark Lynde, who has been my sponsor and friend for more than a decade. Mark and I are nothing alike. He is a hyper-masculine, conservative guy who shoots guns and climbs mountains. I am a wimpy confused liberal who literally rocks on a pillow to bubblegum pop music.

He is an ex-Navy SEAL who had been everywhere and seemingly done everything. He left the service because of hearing issues and bounced around San Diego for a year or two before returning home to Montana. For five years he played lead guitar and sang vocals for a local rock 'n roll band of legendary repute but got tired of alcohol and life on the road. He started going to AA and became a tremendously successful self-taught graphic artist. He oozed charisma. Why is this guy interested in talking with me?

Everything in Billings reminded me what I lost. The hospital I would never work at. The schools I would never set foot in again. The streets where my patients lived. I knew I would be in the papers soon. My biggest secret would become common knowledge for all the people I cared about, and a bunch of people I did not even know. And I had to do it without the coping mechanisms I had used for a very long time. Could I do it? The awful suicidal thoughts were back. Patrick Carnes, who has written extensively about sex addiction, states that a core belief for addicts is that "if you really knew me you would hate me." I always fear that judgement, even after working on this issue for a decade. But the only way to overcome that fear is to take the plunge. I told Mark what my problem was, exactly what I was facing, and how terrified I was that I could relapse or worse.

He took one look at me and said "Let's put our guns on the table. I hear a man, a good man, in a lot of pain, trying to get out of the fog. I will ride shotgun with you all the way, but you must stay frosty. We are flying a mission through dangerous territory; there will be incoming ordinance, but we can survive this mission." I had to call him daily, read the Big Book of AA and attend regular meetings.

Gratitude. I have seen Mark weekly for almost a dozen years. He is my brother. I would do anything for him. We disagree on a lot of things, but that never affects our friendship and our devotion to sobriety. We fly in formation, always stay frosty, and never forget to focus on one mission objective at a time. Great things can come out of catastrophic situations. Thank God I am a drunk or I never would have met my wingman.

The feds were finishing up their investigation. The clinic was tired of people asking whether I was going to return to work and was trying to figure out how to limit the damage to the institution. I felt as if it was all pressing in on me. I was sober but was so scared about going to prison and dealing with the publicity.

I also got more firsthand knowledge of what it really meant to be suicidal. I thought I knew my foe from spending hours listening to others talk about it, and I was certainly familiar with waking up ashamed and hungover and having a transient "wish I was dead" moment. But this was a different beast entire. Tall buildings had allure. I found myself in reverie thinking about the Vista Bridge in Portland. Could I get to the roof of my old building and jump to the parking lot below. Poetic? Maybe just crash the car into a bridge. Even Christ was tired of it all by the end. I knew these were petulant, selfish thoughts but they haunted me that summer. That poisonous "everyone would be better off" lie kept echoing in my brain like an alarm clock I could not turn off.

Bridget always brought me back to reality. She needed me to pull myself together, figure it out, and stop feeling sorry for myself. I was no longer drunk, and for a short time before my sentencing I had freedom. It would be my last chance to travel wherever I wanted, maybe for a long time, so Bridge and I took a road trip, driving from Billings to Portland, then heading south on the Oregon Coast through the redwood forests of northern California to San Francisco, before finally returning home

Every evening Bridget searched online and found the closest AA meeting for me to attend while she watched Harry Potter movies. Only a newly sober alcoholic knows how omnipresent wine, beer, and liquor is when you are trying to avoid it. The future was out of my control, but it was so hard not to obsess. I knew the sovereign remedy needed to escape but between meetings and panicky phone calls to Mark, I managed. I tried very hard not to cry in front of my daughter. It upset her when it happened, but grief comes in choppy waves. We must hold on, let the ocean water break over the stern, and stay on course. I told her truthfully that tears pass, and that I was tougher than I looked or acted, and I knew she needed me to hang in there, and I had every intention of doing so.

Even though it was tinged with the melancholy of anticipation, that Pacific Coast jaunt was the most memorable trip of my life. I had no idea what I had been missing over the previous few years. Instead of spending time with the most delightful twelve-year-old girl in the world, I had spent much of it drunk. Still, we made up for at least some lost time, hanging out at OMSI and the Zoo in Portland, plus Voodoo Doughnuts and gourmet ice cream shops. Perfect days on the glorious Oregon coast, hours hiking in the ethereal silence of redwood groves, then walking San Francisco. We did not talk about the future, we talked about the now. Why *Titanic* was her favorite movie. How kids in her Catholic middle school came out as gay or bi as casually as if they were adopting a new hairstyle. Whether she should be in speech and debate or take up the guitar.

On our last day in San Francisco, I dragged her to Russian Hill overlooking Coit Tower and the Bay, the same panorama which had so impressed me fifteen years before when I pondered what life would look like single and alone. Not even the glimpse of Alcatraz in the distance kept me from feeling almost giddy with happiness.

Gratitude. So many twists and turns in life. Fifteen years ago, I had been in San Francisco seemingly without a care in the world, but alone and miserable. Now I was back, about to have my secret world explode just before I went to prison. But as I inflicted one last annoying hug on Bridget ("Dad, you are so embarrassing, you love me, I get it") I sensed, if only for a moment or two, that amazing grace was real.

I knew it was a brief respite from reality.

On the last day we were in San Francisco, the clinic decided it would pre-empt bad news by sending a letter to all my patients indicating I was going to be federally charged for possession of child pornography. The clinic truthfully stated they had never been aware of my behavior and wanted to support my former patients. They were going to set up a week-end clinic where any of my patients could come if they had questions, concerns, or claims. Later that day, the TV stations procured a copy of the letter. The night before I started driving home from the bay, the reporters came to our cul-de-sac asking to talk with Fran. Neither Fran nor my neighbors had any comment, but it was the headline story in the paper and on the news. I viewed the story that night on my cellphone in the hotel. One of my former patients appeared on the television, her face obscured by shadow to preserve her anonymity.

The only thing I remember her saying was "I thought I could trust him..."

Chapter 14

Court

In early summer, I made my initial court appearance to change my plea to guilty. The district attorney had decided to only throw part of the book at me. There are four charges that can be filed regarding child pornography. In descending order of severity, they are production, distribution, receipt, and finally "simple" possession. They made the decision to just charge me with possession. How one manages to possess without receipt is unclear, but I am grateful for the prosecution's forbearance.

By now, some of the initial scandal started to wear off. I think the newspapers and TV stations realized this was not as juicy a scandal as they initially thought. Despite the publicity, there were no allegations of patient abuse or molestation. Several of my patients' parents wrote unsolicited letters to the *Gazette* acknowledging their disappointment in my behavior while recognizing I had helped their child. My crimes were not the tip of the iceberg hiding more egregious behavior. It was the iceberg and fully destructive enough on its own. I am sure some people wondered if I had committed other crimes, but I had not. The initial fever passed. It is some solace to know how quickly we become yesterday's news.

Court was still humiliating and horrible. It only took a few minutes, but after pleading guilty, I was remanded to the U.S. Marshals to be fingerprinted and to obtain a cheek swab for DNA. The booking room had a helpful poster reminding me of my rights if I was sexually assaulted in prison. I also met with the probation officer who would supervise me until I was sentenced. He fitted me with an ankle bracelet and dispassionately reminded me that he did not care whether I awaited sentencing at home or in jail, it was all the same to him. That day I also met with the officer who was to prepare my pre-sentence investigation. All I could do was tell my story as best I could. Nothing was in my control.

But I was lucky. I had Mark, and I had my meetings. I started seeing Mike Sullivan, a therapist who specialized in treating sex offenders. I had met Mike informally several times during my career. As always, the ignominy of having to discuss my sexual attraction and crimes with a former colleague, someone I had shared patients with, was devastating. I felt like the Benedict Arnold of child psychiatry. It turns out there were resources even in Billings. I wish I'd had the wisdom and courage to seek them out before my world came crashing down, but regrets are of limited utility. Mike has been invaluable to me. Sex offenders need a therapist who is empathic but is not afraid to call us out on our self-destructive tendency to deny and minimize. Just a rock-solid guy, and another model for how to be a genuine man.

Thank God for my PS3 and *Red Dead Redemption.* Of course, I no longer had a computer, but I had gone from working sixty hours a week and filling the other hours with compulsive behaviors to having very little to do but dread the future. I played that video game every day for six straight months. It was the perfect game for me. John Marston, the protagonist, with his own criminal history, is blackmailed into cooperating with a corrupt sheriff to save his family. A sub-plot is his attempt to be a better father and husband to the family he physically and emotionally abandoned during his outlaw days. I sometimes think that the secret to surviving modern life is trying to choose positive obsessions over negative ones. I am not going to claim video games are a perfect way to spend time, but under the circumstances, it was the best I could do, and in its own way, it was an inspiration.

Every once in a while the alarm on the base station for my ankle monitor would go off for no reason. It wailed like the "all hands" alarm on an aircraft carrier. It usually meant that a battery was not charging properly or the base was not dialing my ankle monitor quickly enough. After one minute or two it would stop, as mysteriously as it had started. It could do this in the middle of the night, terrifying poor Fran who thought WWIII had started. I was dead-heading the roses out front once morning, when I get a message on my phone to call my pre-sentence officer "ASAP." Good lord, what had I done this time? "Peak, where the hell are you?" "I am in my front yard, trimming the rose bushes." "The monitor says you are out of bounds, get back in the house, or you will spend the next three months in jail." After that, I did not even take the trash out to the dumpster. I think my basal heart rate was twenty beats higher that entire fall.

I was only allowed to leave the house to go to therapy and AA meetings. Groups of people are scary but individual addicts are almost always kind, and meetings offered an opportunity to work on my defects while staying sober. Not drinking was harder than avoiding the computer. I had nightly drinking dreams where I stumbled about mysterious dark corridors knocking over bottles of wine like pins in a bowling alley. I would wake up shaking, only to be joyously relieved to realize I was still sober. In the short-term alcohol always worked to make everything disappear. And now it was gone. But I knew staying sober was important for my court case and I could see how symbiotically destructive the pornography/wine combination was. Mark talked with me every night: "stay frosty, do not get too up or too down, God is ever-present."

And some things were better. I got to see Bridget and help her with homework every night. We did not talk about the past or the future, both were too hard—but we talked about Harry Potter, politics, and the abiding sweetness and stupidity of our pound pup Sparky. I had always told my patients' parents that quality time is a myth—all the time you spend with your children is important, and I was finally taking my own advice. I also found glimpses of serenity. I spent every noon at my AA meeting and tried to focus on memorizing all the sensations I associated with it, such as the smell of coffee and the shape of the chair I generally occupied. Most of my AA colleagues had been in jail, if only for a day or two. They survived, as would I.

My sentencing was set for December 7th, less than ten months after the investigation. The district attorney was asking for a prison sentence of 26 months, which realistically could have been a lot worse, although it still seemed like an awfully long time. The holidays were coming up, and the district attorney's office repeatedly offered to postpone the sentencing into the new year if we desired, but I wanted to get it over with. I would be investigated, charged, sentenced, and incarcerated within a year. The sooner I dealt with the inevitable, the sooner I could move on from what my twelve-step colleagues reminded me was a valuable "learning opportunity."

My sentencing was on my poor wife's fiftieth birthday. Bridget helped me pick out a new suit. Fran could not come; it was just too hard. Present were a few twelve-step peers and several colleagues that had stuck with me through the whole process. The guys who investigated me in February were there, as well as the agent I had initially contacted. I believe it is so everybody can see the fruits of their labor. Thankfully, no press attended; the thrill was gone.

The basic question was how long I should be incarcerated. I cannot remember very much of it, other than it went better than I could have hoped. The judge reminded everyone what a serious crime this was, but that I appeared to have genuine remorse. I had several supportive letters from respected individuals in the community, and he wanted me to come back and practice under supervision (which I had not expected him to say; I did not think I would ever practice again). He told me I would be doing real prison time, not at a camp or a low security facility, but he was only sentencing me to a year and a day. This was a significant "downward variance" from the usual sentence. There are many parts of the federal justice system I struggle with, but I am very grateful for the kindness shown to me by Judge Shanstrom. It was not just the lenient sentence, it was the fact that he could dislike the crime but see it as a human behavior, and that my life as a "responsible member of society" was not over.

The whole process was an out-of-body experience. The opposing attorney shook my hand, which I found odd. I should have been relieved, since the government wanted two and a half years, but again, all I could feel was deep shame and remorse for the whole sordid affair. There is nothing like looking on the docket and seeing "United States of America vs. James H. Peak" to clarify where you stand in life.

It was just a day or two later I got a letter from the U.S. Marshalls informing me I would be serving my time at FDC Sea-Tac and that I should present myself at the facility by 1:00 pm on January 7th, 2012.

That Christmas was a mixture of hope and melancholy.

Bridget was helpfully researching prison survival techniques.

"Dad, this might be a good opportunity to learn some ju-jitsu and how to handle a shiv. Remember, always be respectful, don't rat anyone out, and never, ever bend over in the showers."

Thanks, sweetheart.

Still, I knew I could survive anything for a year. I got all my life insurance information together, made sure Fran knew she could contact Mark if there was a household emergency, and mentally prepared for my attorney called a "federally mandated sabbatical."

Chapter 15

Sea-Tac

I had four weeks before reporting. I read up on prison to see what it was like and probably watched too many episodes of *Lockup Raw*. I visited with all my friends, one of whom made me a replica of the "Bad Mother F——r" wallet Samuel L Jackson's character owns in *Pulp Fiction*. Fortunately, I was able to "self-report" and fly to Seattle FDC on my own, thereby avoiding the dreaded "Con-Air" system the US Marshalls use.

FDC stands for Federal Detention Center. It was more of a jail than a prison. A prison is where you do long periods of time with an outdoor yard for exercise and some form of daily work routine. Jail is mostly a place where you sit. I did a lot of sitting at Sea-Tac. Seattle is the location for the Ninth District Court of Appeals, and the institution provides inmates with secure housing while they go back and forth to court. It also was a place where people with relatively short sentences could wait out their time.

I flew in the night before and made sure I knew where the prison was before I checked into my hotel. January in Seattle is cold, rainy, and bleak. That evening I binged on a sensible last supper of green olive and pepperoni pizza and Häagen-Dazs.

The next morning, I showed up right on time and was told to take a seat in the cold, featureless lobby. Four hours later an officer called me in. I would not see grass or the outdoor world for the next ten months. Everything in Sea-Tac is rote and dehumanized. It is just the way the Bureau of Prisons (with its delightful acronym "BOP") rolls. My few personal effects were removed. The dehumanizing strip search accomplished. A farcically cursory physical was performed (the physician assistant who performed it told me the best thing about working for the BOP was that nobody cares whether the patient complains). In his sentencing, Judge Shanstrom had mandated a detailed psychological assessment be performed on admission. It took seven seconds and consisted of the following: "Are you currently suicidal? No? Okay, we are done here." Then I was encased in a bright orange jumpsuit about four sizes too big and sent to the unit. The orange signifies you are new; after a day or two, your regular clothes arrive, khakis and simple shirts. Everyone is dressed like Anthony Hopkins in *Silence of the Lambs* but without the mask. I got to the "pod" around dinnertime. I asked someone where I should sit and was told to "Sit with your own kind." I was given the standard plate of mush but had nothing to eat with. Finally, a guard took pity on me and found me a plastic "spork," a combination spoon/fork made of hard plastic not easily transmuted into a shiv.

It was a loud, disorientating place, all cream-colored concrete and steel doors. The CO (commanding officer) showed me to my cell and introduced me to my first "cellie," Robert, an older white guy doing time for security fraud. The officer at intake told me I needed to lie about my crime, or I would be labeled a "chomo" (child molester) and bullied. So, when asked what I was in for, I replied, "tax fraud." One old codger who had been through the ropes took one look at me and smirked, "Nice try, but you can do better." I was terrified. Night finally arrived and I ascended to my bunk. On my left was a window of sorts about four inches wide and two feet tall, but it had been heavily glazed over so you could distinguish day from night, but little else. Someone told me that the glazing had been added because an inmate had gotten hold of a laser pen and tried to use it to blind commercial pilots landing at the adjacent landing strip.

I accrued little sleep that night but was compensated by a subtle yet palpable spiritual intimation. Maybe I was dreaming, but it was not like any dream I've had before or since. I was lying on my cold hard bed, with a blanket the thickness of a tablecloth, in a jail cell for the first time, very alone and very scared. My mind was racing, and I assumed there would be no rest that night. Hours passed. Was I awake or asleep? Slowly a series of two-dimensional images began to materialize in my mind: a collection of remarkable pieces of art, some paintings, others that looked like stained glass. I intuited they were all masterworks, more beautiful than words could express, projected before my mind's eye one after the other, like the Kodak slideshows your uncle inflicted on the family after his trip to Greece. There was no narrative involved— it was not my usual dream where I perceive myself interacting with an imagined world. A typical dream for me involves being confused at school, not knowing what or where my classes are, only knowing I am absent and failing. In those dreams I hopelessly wander long grey colorless corridors. This was utterly different. I was motionless, a simple observer privileged to behold images projected into my consciousness, distinct, polychromatic, of such grace and harmony that they insisted on celestial origin, radiating an aura of love and protection.

I was deeply reassured and comforted.

I chose to interpret that experience as God communicating reassurance, that I would not be abandoned in jail. I also sensed that I had important things to learn here, which I would not learn anywhere else, because I was finally broken and teachable.

Make no mistake, in general, jail is heartbreakingly sad. I was lucky. Although physically the layout was like a medium security prison, politics were kept to a minimum. "Politics" is the prison term for gang/ethnic conflicts that commonly arise when the youngest and most violent offenders are stuck doing hard time. Under those circumstances you must prove to your fellows that you will not be a victim. You can get in danger quickly if you owe money because of gambling or drugs. But no one is in Sea-Tac for more than a year or so, and for short-timers, there is little incentive to get into trouble, and every incentive to get home soon.

Still, you had to keep your wits about you. One area of the pod had an uninhabited cell barricaded by yellow KEEP OUT police tape. Apparently, a young gang member assaulted a CO because he was facing "football numbers" (mandatory minimums of 14 to 21 years) after sentencing and wanted a fierce reputation on paper before he was sent to a penitentiary. I did not see anything like that when I was there, but then I went to great lengths to avoid drama.

The first thing I learned at Sea-Tac was that there are good guys and bad guys, and that everyone on the wrong side of the locked door is in the latter category, and that included me. Greenhorns think it is okay to visit with the officers, and that we should be nice to everyone. I had a kind CO tell me after two days not to ever speak with him again unless he asked me first, otherwise everyone would assume I am a snitch. That was helpful.

The second lesson was that the inmates were just human beings in prison garb, no better and no worse than anyone else. A lot of the guys were illegals from Mexico and Central America, picked up by ICE. Not drug lords, just regular guys trying to make a better life for their family. I was housed on Pod G, which was mellow even by Sea-Tac standards, with a relatively large number of old guys, probably with non-contact sex offenses (you avoided talking about what got you in jail if you were smart), petty crime (one guy sold counterfeit videos) and minor crimes committed on a reservation or national park like drunk driving or illegal trapping. The demographic breakdown was even; about a quarter white, a quarter black, a quarter Hispanic, and a quarter native. Racism is formal in prison; you eat and watch TV with "your kind."

I often felt that the unhappiest people in prison were the officers. As one of them said to me, "Peak, you're lucky, you get out in a year, I'm stuck here until I am 55 (the mandatory retirement age)." There were only one or two officers watching 50 or 60 guys. Most shifts were incredibly dull, but as noted above, officers spent eight hours at a time with bored, devious, and occasionally hostile inmates, every day just like the one before, just waiting for their occupational sentence to end.

To survive, you must develop a routine. I could do that. And if a psychiatrist has any skill at all, it is how to talk and get along. The unwritten rules were simple, but important. Mind your own business. Be respectful. Keep your mouth shut. All an inmate owns is a few belongings and what dignity they can muster. Do not infringe on either. When you urinate, do not miss, even a drop—if you do, wipe it up. Always say excuse me, please, and thank you. Did I mention mind your own business? Sea-Tac was full of young men possessed of a mixture of bravado and melancholy, most initiated into gang activity at a very young age. They were sad, angry, and restless, and wasted their hours playing animated games of poker. You did not want to cross them, since they had relatively little to lose; but if you ignored them, they ignored you. And if you had the chance to talk to them without their homies around, you could see how depressed and vulnerable they were behind the endless muscles and intimidating neck tattoos.

Initially, I thought the self-imposed racialism of the institution was archaic, but in retrospect prison is more honest and open about race than "the outs." Prison has no pretense that it is race blind. But if you are respectful and prove trustworthy those barriers break down over time. It probably would have been different in a higher security institution, where things could get dangerous or volatile quickly and unpredictably. And there was very little for us to do but sit around. We had no yard. The "rec" was just a larger concrete enclosure with windows twenty feet above the floor that let in some natural light. If you were lucky, sometimes you could see the sun or the moon from that skylight, but no trees, no grass, just sky and concrete. You could do burpees (google it), play hoops, or walk the perimeter, which we would do for hours at a time. There were only a few jobs for inmates; I was fortunate to get assigned to the classroom/library, where I taught classes and did some individual tutoring to prepare inmates for the GED. Everything in jail moves in slow motion. Time is all there is, and because there is so much of it, there is no point in rushing. One day dissolves imperceptibly into another. The CO's main job was to look for contraband (for boring inmates like us, it was extra fruit to make pruno—prison wine— or some other silly thing, not shivs or the like) and to tell us to look lively.

What I do know, and treasure about what Tony Soprano would

have referred to as my "correctional experience," is that I made honest friendships with blacks, natives, and Hispanics that I never had before. We make friends with the people we hang out with. Children make friends easily because they go to school every day with the same kids. Young adults make friends easily if they hang out with the people they work with. If you always hang around with white guys, your friends are going to be white guys. If you have the privilege of being around a more diverse group, your friends are going to be more diverse. That is a great blessing. In real life, I stayed in my own lane socially; I could not do that in Sea-Tac, and that was all to the good.

My first cellie Robert taught me the basic ropes, but after just a week or so we all had to go to a new pod so that the toilets in our old pod could be modified to only flush once every twenty minutes, preventing bored inmates from flooding their cells just to raise hell. We were given ten minutes to "roll up" and collect our minimal belongings and prepare to move. The minute I hit the new pod, a huge black guy with cornrows and a Malcolm X tat on his massive left forearm took one look at me and said, "You're my cellie." My opinion in the matter was not solicited.

Derek was from a Portland family where all the men ended up incarcerated sooner or later. His father left home for California long ago. His brother had a sentence of "all day" (life) at OSP in Salem for manslaughter. Derek was finishing up his seven year "beef" with the feds over a drug charge and had been transferred to Sea-Tac to finish up his short time closer to home. Later I asked him why he picked me for a cellie. "Dude, you are an old white guy, and you looked chill. My last cellie was some psycho homie talking shit to hisself all night cause he out of meds. I know we be cool."

Derek did not want any drama for the remainder of his time. He had a psychic spider sense of what was going to happen on our cell block before it happened. His other talents included knowing which COs were "cool" and which were not, when a cellblock shakedown was imminent, what drama was going on elsewhere in the institution, even on the women's side, and most importantly, how to obtain extra cookies. Hustling had been his life from sixteen on, and he had both leadership abilities and entrepreneurial skills. He was a talented barber (always a helpful skill to have on the inside; they do always check to make sure you scissors stay locked at the shop when you leave), but without a license. That required school. School required financial aid. Financial aid required completing a FASFA form (the federal financial aid application) on-line. These things could not be completed before release, but someone could plan for them. Just the kind of thing a chill old white dude like me specializes in. The other option we entertained was opening a food truck back home where he could sell BBQ and his grandma's special cornbread. All the other guys were going to get ahead by rapping, or opening their own tattoo parlor. The Bureau was blithely unconcerned with what happened once guys left. A few make it, but most well, like the Motel 6 guy puts it, "We'll leave the light on for you."

Derek was a stand-up guy, who kept an eye out for me, and who cared about his family. "Cellie, Derek Junior is sassing his momma, I need to get the fuck out of here and kick some ass." I got to put my psychiatry hat back on. "Derek, that is how your dad would have handled it, how did that work out?" "Cellie, if I ever see *that* motherfucker again I will cap his ass."

"Your dad kicked your ass and then abandoned you, let's not do that to Derek, Jr."

Derek looked at me incredulously "Dude, I'm sort of indisposed right now."

"As am I, but we are going nowhere fast. You can still have that conversation; you just have to write." I should have realized that my cellie was functionally illiterate and that writing letters was painful and embarrassing. But I reminded him how much he loved the pictures his kids sent him, and I assured him they would treasure any letters he could write, and that he should consider me his personal editor.

"He doesn't need to see this place, but he needs you. We write him a letter every week. We want to see the art he makes, the friends he has, and the grades he is getting. You think about him every day, but he doesn't know that, but if you write him ten minutes a night, and mail the letter once a week, he will know for sure you are thinking of him. And he will see your handwriting getting better, because you are working hard in school on your GED, and that will make him want to work harder back in third grade in Portland."

We wrote out a list of things his boy could do when he was frustrated, a list of ways he could help his mama, and the name of a book or two father and son could read simultaneously even if apart, and they could share what made the book special. We also made sure every tidbit of Portland Trailblazer news was shared—sports were a great bonding subject. The best we could do, and important. Play the cards you are dealt. Even if it is a pair of threes, improve it if you can, play it if you must, but you cannot fold. I prayed Fran and Bridget read my letters, knew that I thought of them daily, and that I was committed to playing my cards better in the future.

Derek and I were tight. "Cellie, don't tie your shoe on that guy's chair. Its disrespectful, he doesn't want to sit his ass where your shoe has been. Dude doing eight spot in Pipestone, just here for court, if you piss him off he will knock your head off with a lock sock. Dude got nothin' to lose."

Every inmate had a lock for their belongings, if you put it in an athletic sock and twirled it around like a slingshot you could inflict serious damage. Derek helped me avoid those situations. He was a fundamentally decent guy who got shafted in life. I could spend time in self-pity— why did God make me this way, why didn't they give me a break—but at Sea-Tac I realized how much unearned privilege I possessed, and that I had nothing to complain about.

My tutoring gig took up only twenty hours a week, which left a lot of free time. But there were always library books available. Convicts can be well read. I finally got through *David Copperfield*, *My Ántonia*, and *The Sun Also Rises*. One of the few "famous" inmates at Sea-Tac was informally known in the press as the Barefoot Bandit (again, look it up!). I read his copy of *The Count of Monte Cristo*.

I also signed up for a Bible correspondence course. I like school, I like learning. I would have taken up Toaster Repair and Maintenance if it were offered. The courses were designed to encourage an evangelical view of Christianity and to save my sinful soul, but for me it was just an excuse to read the Bible more consistently and systematically than I had ever done before. As a kid I made the mistake of trying to read the Bible cover to cover and invariably gave up somewhere in Leviticus. But these lessons were designed to focus on the New Testament, particularly on the Gospels.

I know there is nothing much more cliché than the prison conversion, but Jesus was just what I needed when I needed it. I felt so ashamed and so dirty for my crimes, a disappointment to God at best and unforgivable at worst. I had never really studied the Bible before, instead only getting snippets here and there, so the overwhelming love of Jesus for sinners was revelatory. Jesus was fully human, and he was well acquainted with humanity. He hated sin but was prepared to offer forgiveness to those who sincerely repented. I know exactly three things about God. First, He is not me. Second, I do not really know whether He exists or what form He (or She) may take. Third, neither do you. But no philosophy makes more sense, and I truly love the Jesus I read about who searches for the lost sheep and rejoices when one is reclaimed.

I would do anything to avoid the tedium and despair of incarceration. I am not convinced the BOP believes in education, rehabilitation, or anything much other than that tomorrow is the same as today and the same as yesterday, but they did have chaplaincy services both in-house and from the community. There were both Protestant and Catholic services weekly. Although I was nominally Methodist, Catholic Mass was the most inspirational service and the highlight of my week. The father who led the service was kind and patient and willing to meet with me on a personal basis about once a month. Since I was incarcerated and there were no mental health services to speak of, he was the one person I could talk to about my existential despair and fear. The lovely artistic images I experienced that first night made me more hopeful that I still had a soul, but some days were worse than others, and I was terrified by the possibility that my life was simply a failure. He told me to offer my sadness and suffering to God as a sacrifice. I grabbed hold of that.

I also went to Mormon services, evangelical Protestant services,

Jehovah's Witness services, anything to embrace a world which transcended prison. But my absolute favorite visitor was Brother Ramon. Ramon held services primarily intended for Sea-Tac's large Hispanic population. Father Matthew was bilingual, but Ramon knew only Spanish, which I knew not at all. Still, his services were open to anyone, and on Sunday anything was better than another episode of Jerry Springer. No one goes to chapel in prison to look good; you go because you need Jesus. For the ICE detainees the service was their sole opportunity to entreat the Lord's supplication. The services were emotional and inspirational. I did not need to know Spanish to follow the essential thread of isolation, sadness, repentance, and a spiritual community with love at its core, and I will never forget it. Those guys also became allies and friends. None of us were winners in this world, but we all had hope for a world beyond the walls. I try never to forget those guys in my prayers. "Blessed are those ..."

Some days were gruesome. If there was conflict anywhere in the institution, you could be unexpectedly locked in your cell for days. Once, while walking the perimeter with my buddies, I almost collided with a CO coming out of a cell he was shaking down. He tried to send me to the SHU (the "hole"), if only because he could, but I was able to talk the captain out of it. The idea that I was a discipline problem was so risible that it was the talk of the pod for a day or two. On one of my short painful calls home, Fran let me know that my dad had passed away. I know my dad loved me, even if he did not like me very much, but it was hard for dad to like anyone other than my mom. I am not sure either of us could have tolerated a truly open discussion about love, sexuality, and what it means to be a man. But now it was an impossibility, an endlessly oozing wound that cannot heal.

Finally, my ten months were up. My friends made me a going away supper of Sea-Tac Surprise. It is amazing what you can create with ramen, meat sticks, processed cheese and hot sauce. For dessert I had a Milky Way. There is nothing that tastes better than a Milky Way in prison, particularly if it is your last night. I wrote one last letter for Derek's family; he would be leaving just a month or two later. It is easy to look up someone's custody status on the BOP web site. I will never look up Derek's name. It would hurt my heart too much to find he was back. My Mexican buddies laid hands and zealously petitioned Jesus' blessings on my behalf. It was one time I was not ashamed to cry.

Fran had sent me some real clothes for the trip home. The facility owed me for my last two weeks of work and since I was at the highest pay scale ($1.08 an hour), I left with forty bucks to my name. One of the kinder COs was working my last day. He reminded me that over half the guys that leave come back sooner or later. I thanked him and smiled, then told him to have a nice life; waited for the last door to unlatch and gratefully stepped back into the green sunlit world.

Chapter 16

Homecoming

Although prison was over, I was not quite home. I still had to serve a thirty-day transition period at Alternatives, the Billings halfway house. Prison was more predictable, and in a strange way, safer. Everyone knew everyone and knew the routine. Alternatives required action; find a job, engage in treatment. You could not just lay on your bunk, read, and do your time.

There were special rules for sex offenders. Unlike other offenders you were not allowed to loiter during regular visiting hours and you were segregated from family and holiday events. There is a heavy melancholy in realizing you are considered more dangerous in public than murderers or gang leaders.

I was back in Montana, the scene of the crime. Everyone now knew the one thing I never wanted anyone to know. And if people asked, I was no longer going to be able to make up a convenient prison lie. At an Alternatives orientation group, I was asked to introduce myself and explain why I was at the halfway house. I told them. The room instantly silenced, and I think the facilitator got nervous. No one expected me to tell that truth in a correctional setting. But I was at the point where if people were freaked out, they could be freaked out. I was done with artifice. I loathe being a sex offender who downloaded child pornography but accept it as a reality and try to muster what dignity I possess to live with it.

Finding a job was painful. I spent five days a week going from business to business, desperate not to meet anyone associated with my previous life while asking for applications. The question "If you are a doctor, why are you looking for a job as a house cleaner (or prep cook or cashier)?" inevitably came up. My medical license was suspended, I was in disgrace and there was no way I could go back to a job in health care. Having a job, any job, is a requirement of federal probation. So I was open to anything. It is impossible not to take rejection personally, but you have to shed it quickly or you might collapse from the accumulated weight. You must always tell potential employers about your crime; talking to someone you have never met about your history is painful but unavoidable. Sometimes they remembered my situation from the news, most of the time they did not want to hear about it. Many would not hire any felons, much less sex offenders. I struck out again and again.

Across the street from Alternatives was the Good Earth Market, our local community-owned organic grocery, and I thought it would be a great place to work, but they had no openings. Still, I worked up my courage and asked if they would let me volunteer until a paid job became available. I also told Perry the general manager how desperate I was to get some structure and purpose back in my life. He thought about it briefly and agreed to give it a shot. Perry's kindness was grace in action. He spoke with the entire staff about hiring me, and whether it made them uncomfortable. Just to be allowed to be around regular people, not locked behind a door was a great blessing and relief. I worked at Good Earth for over a year, and no one hassled me there, not once. God was teaching me that I am not as good as I think I am when I am Good, and I am not as bad as I think I am when I am Bad.

Before I could officially work, I had to complete sex offender registration at the Yellowstone County Sheriff's Department. More fingerprints. The mug shots. Name, address, and e-mail permanently enshrined on the county, state, and federal websites. Mom would be so proud.

Fran hated coming to Alternatives and refused to bring Bridget there—it felt too sad, too creepy, and so shaming. I get it. Jail is supposed to just be for offenders, but if you have a family, everyone shares the punishment to some extent. Several of my previous patients were confined with me. One came up to me while I was in the UA line, happy to tell me he had done better after Pine Hills and prison, and that he was glad to see me. I thanked him while simultaneously wishing I could dissolve. Billings was full of reminders; everything was Before and After. Mortification of the spirit is a necessary and precious gift, but it does not feel that way at the time.

My thirty days passed quickly, and I was home for Thanksgiving. I remember nothing about coming home, finally without an ankle monitor. Part of me just wanted to hide in the basement, but Mark and all my twelve step friends refused to allow me to sulk indefinitely. Fran was relieved. Bridget was more non-committal. I worried about whether she had been harassed at school, but I am the emotionally incontinent one in the family; she doesn't let you see her sweat. She welcomed me home with "So, how was the joint. Were the screws tight? I hope you got a cool prison tattoo." I had federal probation, but I also was on informal Bridget probation. Am I a different person, or is there just another disappointment waiting to happen? She would patiently wait to find out. All I knew is that I was willing to watch *Titanic* repeatedly if I could nestle next to my daughter. Bad news, the film does not improve with repetition. Good news, the ending is perfect.

Sobriety is about focusing on positive distractions and avoiding negative ones. Work was a positive distraction. Good Earth was a grocery-café combination. As tradition requires, my culinary career commenced in the dish pit. It takes a month or two for your hands and forearms to become inured to constant exposure to scalding water. I loved my co-workers, mostly young people working several gig jobs to stay afloat in an unforgiving economy. The store was clean, well run, and served a positive role in the community. Although I had offered to work for free, Perry kindly insisted that I received the minimum wage of $8.75. Initially I liked the job. It was basic and uncomplicated. I soon started prepping salads and making sandwiches. As I told my friends, "The job is not perfect, but no one becomes suicidal if I use the wrong bread." I loved being part of a good organization trying to provide healthy food for the community. I have no problem with cleaning toilets, mopping floors, or waiting tables. Helping is fun. Working to make people's lives better is rewarding. And when I left work, I left work. No phone calls in the middle of the night or impulsive, panicky fears that I had not heard from a patient for a while and had to check in with them to make sure they were safe.

But I was no longer shielded from the public and my history. Some days it seemed that every customer was a former acquaintance, colleague or patient who felt bad for me—and wondered where the ketchup was located. The minute I saw someone I recognized, my heart sank, gloom descended, and I was smothered in a suffocating blanket of humiliation. Perry was always indulgent enough to let me go to the back for a minute or two after I had one of these encounters. Some patients and their families just shot me an angry look, but most told me how much I had helped them, how sad they were when they found out, and that they hoped the best for me in the future. I stammered my apologies as best I could, cried in the back for five or ten minutes, and returned to wipe down the tables. All I can say is it got better over time.

After I had been home for a week or two, I got a call from a *Billings Gazette* reporter. She heard I was back in town. She wanted to talk about my crime and whether I thought I should ever be allowed to work as a physician again. Friends told me nothing good would come out of talking to the press. I did my crime, did my time, and needed to move on and let the world forget. But I had never had a chance to publicly apologize; I just left. I felt my patients and the community deserved an explanation, and I also felt, as bad as my crime was, many other people suffered from my condition, and maybe an honest accounting would be of value. I talked it over with "my two Mike's" (Mike Ramirez of MPAP and my therapist Mike Sullivan) and agreed to the interview. I talked about my sexual attractions and made a public apology for my actions. As of this writing, you can still find the YouTube link for the nine-minute interview on the *Gazette* website. Even though it also made the front page, nothing came of it, good or bad. The people who knew me, already knew me, so this did not phase them. For everyone else it was yesterday's news. People hate talking about this topic and would prefer not to hear about it. I hope at least one or two people found it of value

For the public, sex offender treatment is controversial. It is arguably the most intensive outpatient treatment any offender must complete. There are anger management courses for violent offenders, as well as chemical dependency classes for alcoholics and drug addicts, but none take as long or as emotionally demanding as sex offender treatment. It requires a great deal from both the participant and the provider. But successful completion is a requirement of probation. My group met in the basement of Mike Sullivan's office every Monday night for an hour and a half. There were also weekly individual appointments. We did polygraphs every six to twelve months. Given my alcohol history I also had to submit to regular random urinalyses (UAs) and breathalyzers. I was also under federal probation, so my officer could drop into work or my home at any time.

There were about ten men in my group. There are women sex offenders, but they are so rare that the groups tend to be exclusively men. The ages ranged from 18 to 60. Almost everyone was there for a sex crime against children. The ugly truth is that the sexual assault of adults is rarely reported and rarely prosecuted despite how common those crimes are. The guys in my group were generally blue-collar people, most with a history of "hands on" crime. At first, I was the only one with a child pornography charge, although several would enter treatment before I left. The first thing you hear is introductions, which were scripted and went something like: "My name is Joe, I am 37 years old. My crime is sexual assault of a child in the second degree. I had unauthorized contact with my twelve-year-old niece, including touching of the breast and vagina above and below clothing. I was sentenced to eight years in Deer Lodge (the Montana state prison) with five years suspended. My current assignment in treatment is my written apology to my victim. I am currently working at a food warehouse. Welcome to group."

Group is serious. Virtually everyone was referred by the correctional system and on probation. Not completing treatment often led to a quick trip back to prison. My guess is that in the five years I was part of treatment, about a quarter of the guys finished successfully on the first go-around. Being honest about sex is hard. Being honest about your sexual abuse of children is brutal.

Every offender who is not a psychopath (they exist, but are rare, and do not last long in group) has psychological defenses that facilitates their crimes. We minimize what we did, the consequences that occur, and try to hide our crimes and our guilt. Every offender has a different story. Many come from their own nightmarish history of abuse, almost everyone has drug and alcohol issues, and everyone is trying to live day to day with the stigma and shame. All addicts are liars; untreated sex offenders are profoundly skilled in this area. In his landmark book on sexual addiction, Patrick Carnes correctly notes one of the fundamental beliefs of any sex addict is that "If you really knew me, you would hate me." This belief invariably arises in childhood, and by the time we get to treatment, our protective but ultimately self-destructive shell has had years to thicken and harden. Cracking it open takes time and courage. In a productive group, there are veteran members who persistently and emphatically point out where new members are deceitful or in denial of their problems. That is why the introductions are so uniform, so the offender cannot minimize or excuse their actions.

No one glides effortlessly through treatment. At Sea-Tac I had no access to alcohol, the internet, or even the library. In prison you cannot even watch R-rated movies. Plus, the consequences of my behavior were right in front of me every time I looked at the concrete walls of my cell. But any addiction or compulsive behavior is both patient and persistent. It has not been easy but as of this writing I am ten years away from viewing child pornography, but I have sexual thoughts involving children daily, and I must always fight the desire to look and collect. I will see an ad on TV, or a lovely actor profiled in a magazine. I am walking in a bookstore, and there might be a drawing of a boy on the cover of a teen romance magazine or manga. That starts the maddening itch in my brain, that restless mindless gnawing. It initiates the endless back and forth duel between fear and desire. I know watching pornography is bad, but my attractions are persistent and unchanging, and fifty years of life taught me never to talk about them to others. People like me are used to a life of secrecy and deceit, not because we are intrinsically dishonest, but because experience teaches us it is the only way to survive. Group is about changing that belief system and talking about the things you can never talk about. One of my treasured minimizations is that it is okay to objectify if what you are objectifying is not illegal; I have complicated and conflicted feeling about these issues. But what does not work, now or ever, is "If I pretend to tell you the truth, will you pretend to believe me?"

Group would generally commence with guys discussing their week and it could easily degenerate into a self-pitying bitch session about lousy bosses, selfish ex-wives, and broken-down pick-ups (hunting and pick-up trucks are eternal obsessions for eastern Montana manhood). Mike would inevitably shut down the complaining with "I know, I know; work sucks," followed by; "what is really going on?" Like everyone else, I was confronted on how my thinking had gotten me in trouble and how I would justify my behavior. I did not have hands-on behaviors, but my cognitive errors were just as great as those of my peers, and in many ways, I had a much more comfortable, privileged childhood.

After I had been at group a month Mike introduced Jerry, a new member. Like most new participants, Jerry was not happy to be here. He was an oversized man with coarse features and dirty blond hair, hunched over in one of our modest modular chairs, which I worried was going to collapse under its burden. He came to group right after work covered in car grease and grime. His most prominent habit was making an involuntary little hum whenever he was uncomfortable, and he was uncomfortable a lot. He completely minimized his crime, which consisted of being arrested for attempting to solicit a fifteen-year-old girl. "Yeah, I knew she said she was fifteen, but she didn't look like it or act like it in that chat room, huhmm, never should have got sent to jail, but that f—ing judge Weinsteinberger or whatever, he had it in for me from the start." Mike shut this verbiage down very quickly, but I recognized him as just a grown-up version of the type that teased and tortured me in school. I loathed him from the get-go.

It is so easy for me to judge people, until I listen to their story and remember mine.

He was raised by a grandmother in East LA, in a Hispanic community where he was hassled for being one of the few white guys. Mom worked as a stripper in Vegas, sometimes sent money, usually not. His putative father, as always, was doing time downstate in Atascadero. So lonely growing up. Molested by a female babysitter when he was ten, was it good or bad? He was not sure. Scared of the strange men that would come in and out of his grandmother's house, learned to carry a knife. Brought knife to class, at sixteen got into scuffle with some black kid, got tossed out of school. He is convinced it was reverse racism. Odd jobs here and there, little weed here, lot of alcohol there. Fell into brief relationships, but the woman always ends up cheating, leaving him sad and humiliated. Managed to scrape enough money together to start a modest auto body shop. Found himself spending a lot of time watching adult porn on the computer. Now and then finds himself intrigued with phone sex, but it is expensive and starts hanging out in various internet chat rooms, leading to the charge.

The above paragraph has taken me two minutes to type; it took Jerry over a year to tell it, lots of hemming and hawing, lots of umms and hmms. About the only time he seemed comfortable was talking about his Australian Collie/Pit Bill mix Lila who was his constant companion and looked at him with the same adoring look Nancy used to favor Ronald Reagan with. And I had to give him credit, he hung in there, finishing up a year in Alternatives before he finally got his own little apartment and a decent job towing trucks. He turned out to have some grit, but I still wasn't sure I liked him.

Life settled into a routine. Twelve step meetings two or three times a week. Therapy twice a week. Billings had a modest Caduceus group of recovering doctors like the one I attended in Fort Worth when I was at Santé. Just a couple of dentists and physicians, mostly with drug issues, trying to stay sober while figuring out how to put a shattered life back together. My initial plan was to make an appointment at a public place with one or two of the senior members where I could introduce myself. We agreed to meet at 7 pm at a community church. Once I got there, I was greeted by a dozen young teenagers in pajamas; it was the youth group's slumber party. God has a wicked sense of humor.

There were only five of us in the Billings Caduceus group. Everyone there had been through the wringer in one way or another, and they were all piecing their lives together under the watchful eye of MPAP and the state medical board. We would meet at a local restaurant every other Wednesday and share French fries; kvetching over the struggles of sobriety while dealing with all the personal, economic, and legal consequences of our collective misadventures. Everyone had a story.

After a few months I was not even the newest member or the only one on federal probation. Cathy came to us after spending several months at Betty Ford in California. She was a spitfire blond, smart, passionate, and intense. She had worked for years as a physician assistant at a remote but busy emergency room on the Northern Cheyenne reservation, but like many of us, had a difficult past which she attempted to neutralize with opiates. A patient informed the DEA that Cathy was giving her multiple prescriptions in return for a portion of the pills. She came to us bewildered and overwhelmed. As always, it made the front page; the papers love the disgraced doctor story.

"Eight cops with FBI vests showed up at my house. It is all over Facebook. You are now staring at the Drug Queen of the West End. My poor kids, what will their friends say?" She had three kids living at home from fifteen to five. The little guy, Terrance, was her pride and joy. "I don't know what they are going to charge me with; no one will tell me anything." For a change not only was I not doing the crying, I got to play the role of calm and sweet reason. "Trust me, you are the talk of the town for a week, then everyone moves on to the next scandal, and there is always a next scandal. Now you are sober and going to meetings. The kids might be embarrassed, but it will pass, but if you stay in recovery that will be forever. Waiting while they decide whether to charge you, and what with, knowing you have no say in the matter, is the hardest part."

I knew the ropes. You get fired, your license to practice is suspended. Meanwhile your offense is reported to the National Practitioner Data Bank, where it never can be expunged, your ability to bill for federal insurance is suspended as you are now on the OIG exclusion list, and your DEA number is revoked. At the same time you have no income, mounting legal bills, an unhappy spouse, needy children, and your one reliable if temporary refuge is gone. It feels like a tsunami of misery because it is.

But life goes on, you realize you are more than your job, and even become grateful that you are finally free of the pretense. And you get to give back to others what was freely given to you.

And people can surprise you. Melanie was my probation officer and she promised me she would be happy to send me back to prison if I ever downloaded illegal pornography again, but over time I think she realized I was not Caligula.

Still, I had periods where I was restless and irritable. I want to tell you that I loved washing dishes, that I found it simple but satisfying, a contemplative part of a balanced life. Sadly, no. I liked my co-workers, but when you are in the dish pit, time slows down, like I was back in seventh grade English. The minute you wash one casserole dish, another appears. Sure, I was an accomplished "sandwich artiste" but spending the next fifteen years peeling carrots sounded unattractive. Maybe I could not go back to medicine, but surely, I could do something more productive with my time. I was not eligible to apply to get my license back, but after a year at Good Earth, I started wracking my brains to find more enjoyable work.

It was hard for my former colleagues at the Clinic to reach out to me. It was so sad, and I inadvertently made their lives so difficult. All my thousand or so patients needed another doctor immediately, and they were so busy. The other major mental health provider in town was the Mental Health Center. As doctors, we had always shared call, and Bruce Whitworth and I had spent many days commuting to Indian Health Service clinics at Fort Peck and Crow Agency. He was the first to reach out to me. He spent hours listening to my worries and fears while walking our dogs out on Norm's Island next to the river. He was the one that drove me to my sentencing and wrote a heartfelt and eloquent letter of support. I knew his boss, the Mental Health Center's medical director Tom VanDyk less well. Tom was a West Point graduate and a Vietnam Vet. He had a reputation as a straight shooter, with an unwavering sense of right and wrong. He wanted to sit down and have lunch just a week or two after I got back home. Indulgent Reader, I know you tire of my stories of shame. I tire of telling them, but that was my karma for the first year or two after prison. One apology after another. But Tom reminded me of the good I had done, that he had known me for decades, and would be my ally. When I did petition to get a probationary medical license, he was the one who put his reputation on the line by supporting me, even if it earned him some pejorative comments in the *Gazette*. He helped arrange a volunteer job at the MHC, not involving patients, but volunteering to rewrite their policy and procedures manual, a dull but important task. It got me back to thinking about medicine and policy and out of the dish pit. I loved the people at Good Earth and was so grateful that they employed and embraced me, but it was not how I wished to spend the rest of my life, and they wished me well.

I so wanted to return to psychiatry. It was not the money; Medicaid reimbursement is lousy, and obviously the prestige was gone. But it was the one thing I <u>knew</u> I did well. And I hated to leave the profession the way I did. I knew I screwed up, but I did not feel I was beyond redemption. Just fading away would be the easy way out, but it did not feel right, and for all my caterwauling, in some ways I can be a tough guy.

And I was surrounded by love. If you want to find out who your real friends are, screw up. The people who love you are right there. My neighbors, my therapists, Cathy and my twelve step friends, Mark, Bruce, Tom, I was surrounded by strength, love, and support. And I finally allowed myself to be connected to Jesus's love and forgiveness. I also knew I was not the only pedophile out there, not the only person disgraced. Someone once told me, "If you can't be a good example, be a horrible warning." I thought maybe I could still be both.

Chapter 17

The Board

Years passed. I want to tell you it was easy and everything flowed smoothly. That is not how this goes. My volunteer job at the Mental Health Center consisted of editing an outdated policy and procedure manual which only required Microsoft Word, so no internet access, and just an old flip phone. But the yearning to look was always there.

The most difficult concept for a sex addict to master in treatment is to move past honesty into transparency. Honesty means not lying. Transparency indicates honesty about what is asked, and that nothing unasked is hidden, a considerably higher standard. Every six to twelve months I would take a polygraph. The questions were always the same. First, have I viewed child pornography since my last polygraph? Second, have I had any sexual contact of any kind with anyone under eighteen? And third, did I have any non-consensual sexual behavior involving adults?

The last two questions were easy but answering the first question with impeccable honesty wrapped my brain into more knots than a string of outdoor Christmas lights. If I objectified to any image, did that make it pornography? Is any image of nudity or partial nudity potentially pornography? I have taken over a dozen polygraphs in my life and never failed one, but defining what makes something "pornographic" is subjective, and I could feel guilty just by watching Nickelodeon with Bridget.

I tried to be perfect, so that there could be no gray areas. I could go a month or two without masturbating, which was the purest form of self-denial, the gold standard of abstinence, and the clear goal of all involved. I would think I had these obsessions conquered, but then would see a minor depicted on television or in a magazine and would feel powerfully triggered to browse Wal-Mart or Best Buy, anyplace that might sell desirable films, justifying it by telling myself it was legal, and therefore okay. Sobriety from alcohol kept me from complete dissolution, but that familiar craving, the need to search, to find a magic image, and to disappear into that image, faded but never completely vanished. Some evenings I had "using dreams" where I relapsed on porn, and was sent back to prison, only to wake up in my own bed, terrified and distraught over the ceaseless hold these thoughts had over my mind. I was haunted by a terror that the mournful craving would never abate, and that on my deathbed I would prefer a computer with free internet access above contact with family and friends. How pathetic, empty, and loveless to think that about your soul!

This is when real treatment began, not the repair of my broken mind, but my bruised and battered soul. It required doing two things simultaneously. Relentless focus on transparency in thought and deed, while also developing a more accepting and empathic understanding of my own life and development. Combining both actions is tricky. Transparency demands you are not lulled into temptation by believing the old rationalizations. Simultaneously, you must accept yourself as imperfect human flesh redeemed by a spark of the divine spirit, and beloved of God.

The first part involved trusting Mike Sullivan and telling him of my guilty feelings over buying films, even if no one else knew. I was so lucky to have Mike. He could point out that I was skating on thin ice, and to always play the tape forward. Maybe Behavior A is not crossing the line, but if it leads to Behavior B which does, then I must avoid A. At the same time, he was not so rigid and mistrustful that he always assumed A led to B and beyond. In traditional twelve-step groups like AA, you want absolute sobriety; the whole point is to surrender to the reality you cannot be a normal drinker, with the underlying assumption (which is generally but not universally true) that for an alcoholic casual drinking is impossible and leads to predictable catastrophe. I am not willing to test that hypothesis with alcohol and lose over a decade of perfect sobriety.

Sex and desire are not nearly so black and white. This is a cause of widespread distress and demoralization. Perfection in the treatment of sexual addiction (or eating addictions, for that matter) is a mirage, an unobtainable ideal, worth striving for, but like absolute zero, while you might get close, you will never achieve it. The struggle is the point, a lifelong exercise in honesty and humility.

Is it okay for a guy like me to watch *Malcolm in the Middle*? It is not a simple answer, but I could talk about it, and get honest feedback from Mike and my group without pretending I had no troubling sexual thoughts or behaviors.

And this leads to the essential second goal of treatment; forgiving yourself for being born minor attracted. No zealous prosecutor or vituperative Facebook commenter will ever be able to think worse things about me than I think about myself. I used to alternate between loving my sexuality when it gratified me and loathing it every other moment. Neither extreme makes for emotional stability. I know I am shame-based at my core. I have felt "defective" since early childhood, although it took me decades to identify why and name it. No amount of therapy will make that disappear, but I can and do experience longer periods of peace and serenity where it appears that my life is unfolding as it should.

I told my story over and over; to Mike, to Jerry and everyone at group, to my Caduceus friends. And they still liked me, some loved me. My unhelpful sexuality did not completely define me. I had never been transparent before because if you knew, you would hate me. But I discovered that was not necessarily true, particularly if I was honest about my struggles and was addressing them openly.

Lena was another Caduceus participant working on sobriety while trying to raise two small children, one of which was a toddler whose feet never stopped running unless she was asleep. She also had a newborn son. We were having dinner at our usual meeting place when the toddler decided she wanted to make friends on the other side of the room and tore off at a full sprint. Lena promptly placed the little boy in my arms and took off in hot pursuit. I looked at Cathy in horror. "What is this doing in my arms?" And Cathy sweetly noted, "Jim, she put that baby in your arms for a reason. She wants you to know she trusts you; we all trust you." That pierced my heart. If other people could tolerate the real me, broken and all, maybe I am more than just a loathsome pedophile, and not completely defined by my thoughts. Still, I was happy to get that baby back to his mama before my probation officer walked in the door or anyone else had a chance to make unwarrented assumptions.

I also had many bright penetrating moments of bliss, where I was so grateful just to be alive. In the past, I had put so much emphasis on my title and reputation that I thought I could not survive without them, but the sun still rose in the morning, my daughter still called out "Daddio," my wife and I still loved each other, and I knew who my real friends were. Some people never talked to me again, but that was okay, it was just too creepy for them, but others, often people I only knew in passing, showed themselves to be true blue. God loved me and was healing me through the people He placed in my life. The old me would have found such a concept ludicrous. Why drag God into it? My "rational" brain insisted that He probably does not exist, and if He does, He hardly cares about me, but my heart quietly yet insistently whispers "You are loved, even lowly sin-riddled you." Divine love is the only force that could have changed my life, nothing else makes sense. I am not sure I am capable of loving myself, although I have had several therapists tell me this is the goal of treatment, but I do believe that God loves me, and that is sufficient.

I began to dream that maybe I could get my license back and prevent the professional component of my life from ending in complete ignominy. I did the paperwork requesting a probationary license after the required three-year suspension. The formal response stated that I would have to attend the next Board meeting in person before they would consider my request. My petition was controversial and again made the papers; after all, I was a registered sex offender who had been in prison. One lady from nearby Red Lodge wrote vituperative, caustic letters to the *Gazette* and encouraged the public to attend the hearing to protest my petition. The newspaper wanted another interview, but I had nothing further to say.

Here again, Mike Ramirez and MPAP were my primary allies. Along with helping arrange treatment, MPAP would advocate for me with the Board if I was in strict compliance with all legal and clinical requirements. Upon returning to Billings, I signed a ten-page contract mandating treatment, drug/alcohol testing, polygraphs, and the like. After two years in the community Mike gave me his blessing to move forward with my petition. His support was crucial, and a big ask on my part. Before I left for Helena he reminded me "Jim, if I support you on this and you screw up, the program will never recover." No pressure.

The Board met in Helena. It is an old frontier town, easy to get lost in, even with a small population of 30,000. I arrived the night before the hearing and wandered the streets. One of the city's most treasured landmarks is its beautiful Catholic cathedral. I had not attended services since prison. I feel too dirty, and kids are sometimes in attendance, and I try to avoid kids for everyone's sake. I know I should not feel that way, and that I am not that important or unique, but still. However, I love praying in silence and solitude, and I am so grateful that Catholic churches are almost always open for prayer during the day.

The Cathedral of St. Helena embodies Spirit through its design and construction. It personifies the faith and love of the artisans who crafted the interior and designed the gorgeous stained glass. I no longer believe in a Santa Claus God. I know better than to ask Him for what I want, since what I want is so seldom what I need. But I have learned to pray for others, for His will to be done, and to be given the strength to try to live honorably one day at a time. I had no control over the next day's hearing, I just needed to accept that whatever happened would be okay, and to have confidence that further Instruction would be forthcoming one way or another.

I was not confident I would be allowed to return to practice. Mike reminded me that the overriding mandate of every state professional board is to avoid embarrassing the governor. There was not a lot of precedence for what I was seeking. There was really nothing "in it" for the Board. If they denied my petition, I would be done. A medical license is a privilege, not a right. If I ever re-offended or disgraced myself, the blowback to MPAP and the Board would be immediate and dramatic. The potential "good" would be that I would again be able to provide psychiatric services in a state where those services were in short supply, but that would not make for salacious newspaper headlines.

It was a long hearing, with lots of questions and several lawyers from the state reminding everyone this was a very public review. No protesters attended. I reviewed my crime, my punishment, and my treatment. Mike had put together a list of restrictions on my practice if I was to be re-awarded a probationary license. I agreed to a lifetime contract with MPAP, to never treat anyone under eighteen, and to always have a chaperone in the office. All potential patients would be required to sign a statement informing them my license was on a probationary status, that I was being supervised by Dr. VanDyk, and that more information was available. Under these circumstances, you do not just "get your license back," you must prove your fidelity to a treatment program and attest to your willingness to continue that road. Still, it is a judgement call.

After two hours the vote was unanimous in my favor.

News traveled fast. In fifteen minutes I received twelve congratulatory messages on my antediluvian flip phone. I felt I could float back to Billings. I could not change my past, but I could write a different ending, salvage my career, and defy the nihilistic, self-loathing component of my personality that just wanted to disappear into the basement and play computer games. I had one last chance to change the balance sheet and make some living amends to my former patients and colleagues. I was back in the game.

I was particularly pleased to share my news with my sex offender group, the "lost boys of the basement." So many stories of rejection, thinking you had finally gotten a job only to be told a week later that "corporate" overruled the local office and that no sex offender could ever be hired, being politely but firmly asked to not attend church, being disinvited from the family Thanksgiving meal. As a group, we referred to all the restrictions and all the preconceived notions the world had of us as "The Wall." We earned the opprobrium. We knew why we were surrounded by The Wall. We committed inexcusable crimes against children and must accept the consequences. Not everyone could manage it. We would get guys who could not commit to change, who were too lost in their fantasies, too angry at the world, just too broken. They never lasted. They would try to date single mothers without telling treatment, surreptitiously buy cell phones or tablets to watch porn, or simply deny that they were ever really at fault in the first place, they were just at the wrong place at the wrong time with the wrong kid.

But people could surprise you.

Jerry hung in there. Over months he stopped being so defensive. His boss at the tow truck service was a Mexican American and was kind and generous to Jerry, who became a loyal employee, and stopped making racist comments in group. The goal of group is transparency and vulnerability. For me it meant talking about the pictures of Sascha, and the knowledge I contributed to the exploitation of children, children who were hurt by my support of their betrayal. When I told them about buying films at Wal-Mart, Jerry was the one who said, "ah mm-uh, so are you just gearing up to watch more Russian porn." At first, I flared up, but not only was it a fair question, it was the right question. How do I draw limits, how do I create boundaries that keep myself and everyone around me safe? When am I justifying dangerous behavior? Wrestling with these questions, figuring out how to live a sexually healthy life, is something most men are not prepared to do. It is the absolute last thing we want to discuss publicly. But blade sharpens blade, no one knows the lies and hypocrisy of our disorder better than we do. These are my people. So it was not a huge surprise when I came back to Billings, and Jerry was one of the first to say "Hmmmgh, good job Jim, you made us proud and even knocked a brick or two off The Wall."

Now I had to find a professional job. The natural choice was the Mental Health Center. Their two current doctors were friends, and the practice did not treat children, plus I had volunteered there for a year. It was perfect, and I thought after getting my license, it would be a slam dunk.

The mental health center had several hundred employees and when folks heard I was trying to get a job there, anonymous voices began to express their disapproval. Did they really want a convicted sex offender on staff? Were they sure I had not molested children? (It is hard to prove a negative.) The hire had to be approved by the Center's Board of Directors, which consisted of all the county commissioners in the Center's catchment area. They are elected politicians. At the same time, the Center needed doctors, I was willing to work for virtually nothing, and the whole point of the Center is to provide these services. So, after being pleasantly surprised by the Medical Board, I was unpleasantly surprised by the Center's executive officer telling me in no uncertain terms that I would never be employable at her facility. My well-oiled strategy was now off the rails. I had prayed at the Cathedral for His will to be done; this would be an excellent opportunity to prove whether I really meant it.

All the horrible doubts came rushing back. I felt as popular as an original thought in a Baptist seminary. I had felt so good in Helena; people trusted me. Then a month later it seemed the world had changed its mind. This is where all those years of work made a difference. I could hear Mark remind me I had to stay frosty. Another learning opportunity has presented itself. Just because this was not meant to be did not preclude a way forward. I was temporarily staggered, but I had been through worse.

What were my other options? Obviously, I was never going back to my previous employer. Perhaps Riverstone, the county health clinic for the uninsured and homeless. I figured they were always desperate for psychiatric consults. But turns out they were not that desperate. Maybe the VA? Again, they had a clear need. Soldiers were flooding back from the Persian Gulf with incapacitating PTSD, often suicidally depressed with acute psychiatric needs. But a registered sex offender was a bridge, or maybe several bridges too far. How about the local drug and alcohol treatment center? I knew the docs working there; and after my personal experience, I was certain I had something to offer. I talked excitedly with the CEO several times, but again, once it got to their Board it was a no-go.

My last hope was the State Hospital at Warm Springs, not a job I was keen on. I did not mind working with the sickest patients, but Warm Springs is an isolated community 250 miles from Billings, and I was not going to move. I knew a former colleague who worked there seven days on, seven days off, so I knew it was doable. Most of the staff were locum physicians who would come in for a month or two and move on. The hospital was always recruiting. Mike Ramirez knew the medical director at the hospital and talked to him about me. I called him twice to explain the situation. He knew I was a good doctor and was very excited about hiring me. I knew it would be a hard job with very sick patients, but I was up to the challenge. A formal itinerary for my interview was set up for a Wednesday.

On Tuesday afternoon I was all packed up for the drive out to Warm Springs when the medical director called and told me his boss in Helena overruled him. No job offer would be forthcoming. The hire was just not worth the potential negative blow-back. I was devastated. No one wanted me under any circumstances. The stigma was too great. Not even the grace of the licensing board was sufficient. There was no getting around it, my history was just too toxic for any institution, public or private.

If I was going to make this work, I would have to do it on my own.

Chapter 18

Wood Duck

Opening my own practice was not my first choice, but rather a last resort. Private practice, long the paradigm for American psychiatry, is going the way of cassette tapes. There will always be a throwback or two, but most physicians are employed by a clinic or hospital, usually with a staff of nurses, receptionists, and office managers.

But if no one else would employ me, I would have to employ myself. I picked the name Wood Duck Psychiatry from my wife's self-anointed moniker of "The Duck." On a cold, rainy London day we sought refuge at a pub called "The Dog and the Duck." This was before Bridget, when it was just the two of us. Fran thought it was the ideal moniker for us; she always called me the "dog" because I love going on walks and am loyal and affectionate (sometimes!), whereas she always referred to herself as the "duck," appearing to float calmly on life's pond, while paddling frantically underneath. Wood ducks are singularly beautiful, and I thought it would make a memorable name for a practice.

Nothing was easy. I learned that obtaining my license was just the beginning of the maze of paperwork. I was fine with a mostly Medicaid and Medicare practice. That group included the sickest patients with the fewest resources, the whole point of going back to work. But to receive reimbursement required lengthy applications and everyone needed an explanation of my charges and my practice restrictions. I also needed a DEA number to prescribe controlled substances. I thought that would be easy. I had legal issues, but nothing involving improper prescribing or drug addiction. So I checked "no" when the DEA application asked about legal issues. I should have read more carefully. They wanted to know if I had lost a license for "any" reason, not just drug and alcohol issues. I got an extremely unpleasant e-mail response to my application noting that the agency "knew all about me" and wondering why I had lied on an official federal application. When I tried to explain it was an innocent mistake, they did not buy it; my application was put on hold until they could "investigate further."

I was also discouraged when Medicare, the federal program which provides insurance for both the elderly and the disabled, ruled that enrolling me as a provider would be "detrimental for the program." I lost my appeal of that decision, and I think the judge in the case had the novel pleasure of being able to inveigh against the evil of child pornography. Even though I had agreed never to see children again, the administrative law judge believed my crime precluded safe practice. Her opinion noted "child pornography may not be the worst in the depressing panoply of crimes against children, but it is a serious crime . . . I am deeply concerned that, after eighteen months with a probationary license, Petitioner's license could become full and unrestricted ... and likely to engage in conduct detrimental to the best interests of the Medicare program and its beneficiaries."

It really did not matter that I could never practice without working with MPAP and the Board; for her I was unredeemable as a physician.

That was a significant setback, as it prevented me from receiving reimbursement from Medicare, which is the major coverage for patients with schizophrenia and other major mental illnesses. It did not prevent me from seeing these patients; it just meant I would not get paid for them. I still accepted several Medicare clients, usually previous patients who were now adults. I charged $40 a session, which was hard for the patients, and did not even cover my expenses, but it was the best I could do. I could have made a second appeal, but it would be heard in Washington D.C., and Jay figured it would cost about $80,000 in legal fees, so I gave up. The only practical consequence of the judge's ruling was to make it more difficult for the sickest adult patients to get psychiatric care. She was right; I did get my unrestricted license back eighteen months later. But I saw a lot fewer Medicare cases than would have been better for my practice and for the community.

Fortunately, Medicaid is a state program, not administered from Washington, and the state desperately wanted access to care. I had a reputation as a good provider and my practice had plenty of safe-guards. When I finally got the e-mail that I had been accepted and enrolled as a Medicaid provider, it guaranteed that I could have a functioning practice and see regular folks. Without Medicaid, no one who needed my services could have afforded them.

Still, it was a bit overwhelming. I sent out a letter to former col-leagues telling them about the practice. But I wondered whether there would still be a place for me in Billings. My next-door neigh-bors Sue and Cherry wanted to help me out by throwing an open house. I was hesitant. Who would come? And could I face the Billings mental health community, who I had disappointed in such a spec-tacular way? But Sue and Cherry loved me and loved my family and wanted to show their confidence in me. When I said maybe we should not pressure people to show support, they simply said they were not going to take no for an answer. I had found an of-fice a mile or so from my house—not too fancy, not too run down, a setting I thought would feel comfortable to most everyone. We sent out about thirty invitations. Sue and Cherry made cakes and cookies. It was a Friday night, and I really did not expect more than a handful of people to attend.

More than sixty people showed up. In Billings, among the people who had known me for twenty years, there was so much accep-tance and understanding. It was breathtaking. Most of these were folks I had not seen for months. The fact they still believed in me made my heart ache with happiness and gratitude.

Coming back was the hardest thing I ever did professionally. About a year earlier, while I was still at Good Earth on one of my sol-itary walks I spotted my old friend Kee passing me by in her sporty red Audi convertible. Kee had "kid magic," the uncanny ability to listen and connect to my most troubled patients. She was the most talented child therapist I have ever known, and I steered as many patients as I could her way, even though it upset the clinic since she was in private practice. But I did not care where you worked, only if you were good. I called her all the time at the end of a long day with the same line "Kee, I have one for you. You are gonna love this kid, but it's a tough case ..." She never turned me down.

We had dozens of patients in common when I fell off the face of the earth. How many difficult conversations had she had with shared patients on "what the hell happened to Dr. Peak?" I knew I could reach out, that I should reach out, but I just could not face her. Kee was not just magically effective and charismatic, she was transparent and real. She had dealt with her own issues surrounding sexuality, was in a happy long-term relationship with Stacey, and was a great mom to the son they shared. She navigated treacherous waters with nerve and skill. I capsized.

So my heart sank when that Audi stopped on a dime, fishtailing back to intercept me on my ramble, knowing I would have to make yet one more hopeless fumbling apology, one more attempt to explain the unexplainable and excuse the inexcusable. She stopped that Audi so fast it left tread marks. "Jim, I am so happy to see you. We have been so worried." I try to mumble some hopeless sort of apology, but what do you say? "I'm sorry, tell the kids I am so, so sorry ..." "Jim, honey, they all miss you and are sad for you, but they are ok, I told them you are getting help, they just want you to be better. I am so happy to see you again, when are you going back to work, we need you." I told her I was not sure I could ever go back, but happily agreed to meet with her every week at Perkins at the ungodly hour of 7:30 to let her know how I was doing. We met every Tuesday for three years, for what was essentially free therapy.

I wanted so bad to be back, but it was a new world. I was on my own, and terrified. A convicted, registered sex offender opening a new practice. Could anyone ever trust me again? I had dark visions of protests and graffiti on the walls. Kee reminded me I was catastrophizing. All the patients she worked with; felt bad for me, but were not angry at me, certainly not as angry at me as I was at my-self. Kee was one of the people who came to that first open house and gave me the encouragement to believe I could do it. Whenever an obstacle would appear such as hospital or an insurance provid-er not working with me, or a patient not knowing why I wouldn't prescribe all the meds she wanted since "everyone knows you are an addict yourself," Kee would patiently walk me through each snare step by step. Some mornings I felt paralyzed; I just wasn't sure I could do this, terrified I would screw it up yet again. We talked a bit about my old patients, how they were, and whether I was re-deemable. I went through napkin after napkin because I can never talk about previous patients without tears. Our server learned to leave an extra one or two at our table the minute we sat down. And almost by magic, it slowly got easier.

Previous patients came back, and I was so happy to see them. New patients with drug and alcohol problems found their way to me. Colleagues who remembered me fondly made new referrals. It was a good mix. Every now and then someone would bring up my past crimes, often in the context of their own abuse. All I could do was tell them the truth as best I could, then let them know I cer-tainly understood if they were not comfortable working with a sex offender. I may have lost one or two patients over seven years, al-though I am sure many people chose not to work with me because of my history.

It could be lonely work. Lori was my faithful office manager for over five years, and I think we ran a tight ship. At MPAP's request, a window was inserted between my office and the waiting room so that no patient was seen behind closed doors. I also had a great su-pervisor in Dr. VanDyk and many friends and supporters, knowing in the end only you can make the tough judgement calls on how to handle tricky situations with limited backup. Solo practice is very daunting work. But we had a lot of fun, and I think people felt safe and cared for in our little office.

Nothing was easy, but nothing is supposed to be. I was very good about avoiding pornography, but my attraction never goes away completely. I would still check out video stores now and then and buy a film or two with younger male protagonists. It was a lot more benign than where I had been before. I was honest about it with treatment; the goal was to give myself a chance to have some form of vaguely healthy sexuality without going down the rabbit hole of old habits. A film I loved was *Estreros*, a gay romance involving two teenagers. No nudity, some implied sex, but nothing remarkable. You could get it on Amazon. I loved watching it. I thought it was a reasonable compromise.

I passed all my quarterly polygraphs, although I always found the experience nerve-wracking. I was in treatment and doing well, but was hypervigilant about people "knowing" and becoming offended. Every month I would fill out my report of supervision for my probation officer. I did UAs three to four times a week, at Alternatives. Every morning for five years I woke up at 5am because that is the earliest you can call to see whether you need to test. I submitted forms regularly to MPAP, the Board of Medicine, and a copy of every script I wrote to the DEA, who, thanks to my federal probation officer's gentle prodding grudgingly restored my controlled substance license. I attended four to five hours of treatment weekly. I was happy to do it, as it was infinitely preferable to pressure washing casserole pans. The only struggle was realizing how many eyes were on me, and the daily weight of living as an offender. What did I do if a patient brought her child in to wait while I saw her? Lori was supposed to always be in the office, but even she needed a break now and then, and patients would often drop in after hours. Folks could not understand why Medicare would not cover my services, no matter how many times I explained it. Some private insurances would cover my practice, others wanted nothing to do with it.

Other hurdles were surmountable. I was able to obtain private malpractice insurance, at three times the going rate despite the fact I had never been sued. After several letters I was readmitted to the American Psychiatric Association. After three years of supervised practice, I was allowed to retake my Boards in Adult Psychiatry. Slowly, one step at a time, I built a practice, but I always seemed to be looking over my shoulder, waiting for the other shoe to drop.

Melanie got promoted, and the quality of my officers dropped off quickly after that. About once every two years, the SWAT team shows up to your house to perform an unannounced sex offender round-up to make sure everyone is where they are supposed to be. It is never a good sign when a guy with a shotgun and a combat vest drops by with a team of cops, but I got as used to it as I could.

I went over a year without ever seeing anyone from probation. Now and then I would get a form letter indicating Officer X or Y had transferred to Missoula, wished me the best while informing me I would be hearing from a new officer soon.

So, it was a surprise that one day after treatment, I found a group of three federal probation officers ransacking my house. Fran was horrified; had I screwed up again? Were they concerned I had a caged altar boy stashed away in the basement? No, they were just going through my movies. After an uncomfortable hour or so of Fran and I looking at each other, the grim leader finally emerged up from the basement holding my copy of *Estreros*.

One on one officers are usually okay, but when they arrive in a pack, and they are all guys, I think they compete for who can be the most shocked and appalled that people like me exist. The one in charge, generously armed, covered in camo and patriotic insignia motioned me over.

He held *Estreros* from its corner with his pinky and index finger as though it is covered in slime. "What is this?" "It looks like a film." "Is it yours?' "Yes." "Should you be watching this—are you still attracted to teenage boys?" "Well, you know this is kind of who I am." "But is this movie good for you?" "Well, I do not think it is particularly bad for me." "Really? I do not agree." Long silent pause here. "Do you think about sex every day?" "Um, yeah." "Involving minors?" I tried to change the subject, realizing I was playing a game I could not win. "I just passed my poly. I am not breaking the law. I am doing the best I can." Cop #2, his firearm poorly concealed under his flak jacket, sadly commiserated about how hard it must be to have daily sexual thoughts, and he was glad that did not describe him. Apparently they screen out individuals with vigorous sex drives from the Department. "I'm sorry, I just seem to have been born this way."

Meanwhile, the third guy was on his haunches going through my copies of "The Sopranos" next to the upstairs TV while reminding me that they are just there to help. They wanted to know why I was "obsessed with childhood." I did not know how to answer that question, other than to say I just am, although I am obsessed with a lot of things, including WW II, alphabetically organized pop music CDs, and the Cleveland Browns. "Have you been hanging out at the park and the school playground, checking out the neighborhood kids?" "I am never around kids." (I never am. I know it creeps people out. I love kids, but they do not need me, and the best thing I can do for children at this point is to write this book and leave them be.)

They look at Fran with a mixture of sadness and contempt. She tries to tell them she thought I was doing well, but they imply she is gullible at best, complicit at worst.

Cop #2 asks "Do you want to go back to prison? Why aren't you honest with your therapist about your ongoing deviant behaviors?" Camo hat guy wonders whether I am using a bit of ganja while he mimes taking a puff from an imaginary blunt, which reminds him they need a UA. So we decamp to the bathroom. It is taking a while as I am a bit shaken by this point. "Jim, what's your problem, we don't have all day here."

It was interminable, condescending, and utterly terrifying. They confiscated *Estreros* in a carefully labeled evidence bag as if it was sarin and finally left. Fran commented "Well Peak, it is never dull with you around." She was initially convinced I had broken some huge rule of probation, but nothing came of the encounter.

I never saw any of those guys again.

But I was a wreck for the next month. Those unbidden intrusive suicidal thoughts returned. Jump off a building. Drive into the river. I never seriously entertained them, but when triggered, my shame crashed over me like a tsunami. Group helped. It was the one place I could vent about being objectified as just another scum-bag sex offender. Jerry reminded me, "Uh, Jim, it's just their job, I know it sucks, but you shouldn't have movies like that around; it just gets them excited." I replied with "But there was nothing really bad in that move. I just passed my polygraph two weeks before."

"Ummm, now you are just being defensive and making excuses for yourself. But you are usually calmer than this; are you going to be okay this week?" I was used to worrying about everyone else; it was novel to be the subject of concern. Mike and the group insisted I call someone in my inner circle every day for a week. It was weird but oddly comforting to be the sick patient instead of the psychiatrist. When I talked about it with Mark, he reminded me to "Stay frosty and stay on the trail. Jim, trust me. I am a sailor. Every man, I mean every man has disgusting thoughts. But not every man has to admit what they are. You freak those guys out, because they are just as nasty as you, but in different ways, and that scares them. Keep working in treatment, but remember we fly in formation, and I am on your wing. Stay away from the internet, stay on the trail, one step at a time."

If you are as broken a person as I am, you must work hard to stay in balance, particularly if you are seeing patients. You do not want your own issues to bleed into the issues of your patients, but that requires considerable self-awareness, often learned by working with others. And I had the stabilizing trust of so many people who cared, and knew I was not the same man I was twenty years previous.

The best gift of treatment was to permit me to be a decent father. Bridget is a light, a good friend, and a great kid. We spent a ton of time together after I was released. She deserved a father who was present and genuine. That only emerged after a lot of work, but we can make it through tough times if we have faith and family. That sounds so corny and trite as I type this, but the truth sometimes is.

When I first got back in practice, a lot of my first referrals came from the state's child protective branch. Not the children in care, but their parents. Like many other states, Montana's child welfare system has been overwhelmed by a torrential influx of cases caused by drug addiction. Our state has been particularly impacted by methamphetamine, or "crank," and it is a scourge for young parents. Many users had underlying mental health issues; many were abused kids grown up. Breaking the cycle of generational trauma is hard.

Those parents quickly became some of my best and favorite

new patients. I know what it is like to have shameful secrets and addictions. "I can't believe a child psychiatrist watched child pornography" sounds vaguely similar to "I can't believe a woman would use drugs when they are pregnant." Treatment works, not for everybody, but for more than you might think, and I could play a role in that. Plus, it let me make amends by helping children again, even if I never saw them directly. Several of my patients were referred by the Yellowstone County Family Treatment Court, an innovative program designed to pull all the community's assets together to get kids safely back home to sober parents. People on the team included a judge, a county attorney, attorneys for the parents, attorneys for the kids, probation officers, treatment providers, and therapists, all with a common goal of reuniting families, if possible.

I know people can change. But I also know how hard it is to battle addiction, how shameful it is to know you are hurting children— yours, and those of others—through the selfish but seemingly irresistible need to feel ... something, anything other than the way you feel right now.

I was asked to attend court on behalf of a client and explain my plans for treatment and what I thought she needed from the community to safely parent once again. It was painful to be back in a court room. I felt like an imposter. A part of me almost expected the bailiff to escort me back to jail after I finished discussing the case. Imagine my surprise when the judge asked if I would be willing to be a permanent part of the team, a role I am proud to have served for over four years.

It was so gratifying to be back on a therapeutic team. The court has permitted me to bring what talent and experience I possess to aid afflicted families. My favorite role is talking about what recovery can look like for our participants, and the difference it can make for their extended families, particularly their children. To that role I bring some credibility. When I tell our clients sobriety will give them a new freedom and a new happiness, I mean it, heart and soul.

Chapter 19

Last Call

I have no big fireworks display to end this narration. I am pleased my career ended more with a whimper than a bang.

I practiced at Wood Duck for over six years, saw hundreds of patients and stayed out of trouble, which was exactly my goal. I finished my treatment with Mike Sullivan and bid adieu to my group. Slowly, almost imperceptibly, I evolved from being the new guy in Caduceus to becoming the veteran that supports the newcomer. At our last annual Caduceus meeting in Kalispell, I got to reminisce with Cathy and Lena. Lena finished treatment and realized addiction medicine was her passion; she now heads a graduate fellowship training program in Chicago. Cathy got her license back and heads the emergency room where she had first been confronted by DEA agents eight years ago. Her adorable son developed leukemia, but if we have learned anything it is taking life one day at a time, and he is now in remission.

I petitioned the court to be terminated from probation in July 2017. Except for my *Estreros* incident, I had not received a home visit for almost two years. However, the Justice Department opposed my motion. I still find it a bit curious they put more effort into opposing my petition for termination than they ever did in supervising me. But I realize that investigating and prosecuting sex crimes involving children must be one of the most emotionally and spiritually draining occupations out there. The bar for terminating supervision must be high.

Constructed at a cost of eighty million dollars, the new court-house is a testament to the wary relationship between government and the governed. It is less a public space and more a foreboding security bunker. On the fifth floor is the actual courtroom itself, designed for maximal intimidation. The judge's seat is elevated; she literally looks down on you from beneath a greater than life-sized U.S. District Court Seal. Sound is baffled. Light is natural, but diffused, like a dimly lit basement. I kept looking for Dementors. The district attorney explained to the judge that the Department felt I needed the "support and assistance" of probation for another five years, reminding everyone easy revocation of probations with subsequent re-imprisonment is the ultimate motivator, knowing my underlying nature had not changed.

Being a federal judge is a brutal job. I would rather scrub latrines using a toothbrush than take on that moral responsibility. When the judge delivered her decision, it took me ten minutes to figure out whether she had decided to rule for or against me. On one hand here is the crime; on the other the defendant has done well. On one hand supervision is helpful; on the other the defendant is correct that supervision has been inconsistent. Finally, it became clear that I was off the hook. On the way out the door, I picked up my daughter's computer which had been confiscated on my last visit, even though it was locked. Of course, nothing was on it. In some small way I left the court feeling "freer" than I had in years.

I continued to soldier on for a few more years until, like so many, I contracted COVID in the fall of 2020. Although I was not hospitalized, I felt awful but still had to go to the office every day to deal with the daily routine of prescriptions and emergencies, knowing it was all on me. It was exhausting and endless. Writing just a few scripts used up all my energy. I recognized it was time to leave. There was nothing left to prove. I could leave the field on my own instead of being forced out in disgrace.

I want to personally thank you for reading this. It is a gift to me that you would invest your time walking this road with me. I pray it will be of benefit to someone else out there, so that the path does not have to feel so lonely, and the trail so poorly marked.

Strangely, I have come to recognize the gift that comes with my broken sexuality. I am less arrogant, less judgmental. I still volunteer at our Family Recovery Court, and I hope I never forget what it is like to be on the other side of the bench, humiliated, bewildered, and defeated.

On the addiction front it has taken years, but I am free from the nightmarish desire to die in front of a computer screen. I do not know when the feeling slipped away, but it did.

I think of my life as a small miracle. I was born destined to die a fraud at best, a fiend at worst. It is not a path I would have taken willingly. There were moments of pitch black. But the view on the other side is so lovely that I can be grateful for what I learned in the dark.

I think the thing that really saved me was the example of my young patients, who were able to confront their demons, look at their pain, and provide living examples of resilience and courage. I could not abide being so base and cowardly given their strength and character. And God kindly intervened in the corporeal form of the justice system, granting me opportunities to learn genuine humility, and to meet wonderful people I would not have encountered any other way. I know there are many who love me, the real me, even with my flaws, follies, and brokenness. What a fortunate man!

Still every now and then, when everyone is asleep, I will get out my ancient iPod, close the door to my den, put down a big pillow, and with my adoring puppy beside me, rock back and forth on my rug while thinking how wonderful it is to be playing in a band with Julien, looking forward to a life of love, promise, and innocence.

Acknowledgements

The author wishes to thank all the people who assisted with this manuscript, particularly my editors Russell Rowland and Maxwell P. Sinsheimer.

Many friends and supporters read the manuscripts and made valuable contributions. I am indebted to them all.

I also wish to acknowledge everyone: friends, relatives, therapists, probation officers and peers who helped me to endure my "dark night."

Lastly I wish to extend my eternal gratitude to my patients and their families for their kind teaching and inspiration.

About the author

James Peak is a retired Board Certified Psychiatrist.

He lives with his wife Fran in Billings, MT.

This is his first book.

You can learn more at his website: stupidbrain.com.

www.ingramcontent.com/pod-product-compliance
Lightning Source LLC
LaVergne TN
LVHW041317080426
835513LV00008B/500